When a Family Pet Dies

of related interest

Children Also Grieve
Talking about Death and Healing
Linda Goldman
ISBN 1 84310 808 9

Talking with Children and Young People about
Death and Dying
A Resource Book
Second Edition
Mary Turner
Illustrations by Bob Thomas
ISBN 1 84310 441 5

Without You – Children and Young People Growing Up
with Loss and its Effects
Tamar Granot
ISBN 1 84310 297 8

Lost for Words
Loss and Bereavement Awareness Training
John Holland, Ruth Dance, Nic MacManus and Carole Stitt
ISBN 1 84310 324 9

Understanding Your Three-Year-Old
Louise Emanuel
ISBN 1 84310 243 9

Understanding 6–7-Year-Olds
Corinne Aves
Foreword by Jonathan Bradley
ISBN 1 84310 467 9

Understanding 12–14-Year-Olds
Margot Waddell
ISBN 1 84310 367 2

When a Family Pet Dies

A Guide to Dealing
with Children's Loss

JoAnn Tuzeo-Jarolmen

Foreword by Linda Tintle

Jessica Kingsley Publishers
London and Philadelphia

First published in 2007
by Jessica Kingsley Publishers
116 Pentonville Road
London N1 9JB, UK
and
400 Market Street, Suite 400
Philadelphia, PA 19106, USA

www.jkp.com

Library of Congress Cataloging in Publication Data
Tuzeo-Jarolmen, JoAnn, 1945-
    When a family pet dies : a guide to dealing with children's loss / JoAnn
Tuzeo-Jarolmen ; foreword by Linda Tintle. -- 1st American pbk. ed.
    p. cm.
Includes bibliographical references and index.
    ISBN-13: 978-1-84310-836-8 (pbk.)
    ISBN-10: 1-84310-836-4 (pbk.)
    1. Pet owners--Psychology. 2. Pets--Death--Psychological aspects. 3.
Bereavement--Psychological aspects. 4. Children and animals. I. Title.
    SF411.47.T89 2006
    155.9'37083--dc22
                                                        2006019501

British Library Cataloguing in Publication Data
A CIP catalogue record for this book is available from the British Library

ISBN-13: 978 1 84310 836 8
ISBN-10: 1 84310 836 4

Printed and bound in Great Britain by
Athenaeum Press, Gateshead, Tyne and Wear

Dedicated to Sonny
1991–2005

Contents

Foreword

If you are holding this book, you are trying to help a child whose beloved pet has died. I lost my first dog, Prince, when I was an eight-year-old child. If I close my eyes, I can still hear the clinking of his collar and tags as he walked away down the hallway after our good night ritual. I associated him with comfort, safety and love. And I sobbed myself to sleep for many nights when he had to be euthanized for uncontrollable epilepsy. As a young teenager, I was given the decision of whether to euthanize my two-year-old Great Dane when he bit my girlfriend in an unprovoked attack. I held Bandit as the veterinarian euthanized him ten days later until I was told to go comfort my mother who was standing nearby and hysterical with grief because "she needs you more." I remember the resultant anger and outbursts that seemed so out of character to my teachers and family. Dr. Jarolmen brought so much of that back to me vividly as I read her book. These childhood losses can have life-shaping impact. Adults can help guide and comfort the young bereaved by understanding the path of grief and mourning that they may travel as described herein.

We cannot avoid death. Every hello has its own built-in good-bye. If we open our hearts to love and relationship, we must someday face its loss. Our pets don't live as long as humans and those with companion animals may suffer this loss many times. For many people, the passing of a childhood pet will be the first time death smacks you in the face upfront and personal, as they say. Coping with the child's grief is often difficult for parents who may also be dealing with their own painful feelings about the pet's death. It may make parents uncomfortable as they grapple with their own answers to the basic questions of life, death and what may or may not follow that are raised by the child. You are reading this book because you want to help a young person learn how to move through the process of death and loss. Familiarizing yourself with the information in this book will help you be present for your child openly and honestly. Remember that there are times when wisdom lies in seeking the help of an experienced, caring, professional like psychotherapist JoAnn Jarolmen because you as the parent may be too overwhelmed or the wounds too great. As a veterinarian for 25 years, I have witnessed in my clients, their children and personally all the variations of dealing with pet loss that Dr. Jarolmen describes.

Euthanasia is a complex subject but I try to hold at the forefront that the word means "a good death." Sometimes the kindest choice we can make for a much loved pet is the gift of a good death. Euthanasia can also be one of the most difficult farewells to accept and is a frequent source of guilt that should be discussed openly. However death arrives – quietly, cataclysmically, expected or unexpected – the reality of it must be acknowledged for whatever it is and what it means to the person left behind.

I nodded in understanding and agreement while reading Dr. Jarolmen's chapter on "replacing" a pet. I tell my clients you can never replace a beloved pet but when you are ready, you can fill an aching void. Only you and your family can know when this is.

Be there for the child in heartfelt sympathy and listen. Mourning is different in every individual, is unique to each relationship, may vary with what is going on in the present moment, intersect with other losses, and finds its own road in its own time. It is never easy but it need not be crippling. May this book help you bring comfort and lessen suffering.

Linda J.M. Tintle, D.V.M.

Chapter 1

What Does it Mean
to Lose a Pet?

Reflection: I Will Never Forget His Love
Anonymous Author

Let me begin by telling you that Moby Dick began his life as a feral cat on the campus of Ramapo College in Mahwah, New Jersey. Ten years ago that was a haven for feral and abandoned cats who had been left by overzealous students who had no plans for a pet in their future when they left college. Moby, or Old Taffy as he had been known up to the time when we met, had a reputation with the girls and thus many of the other felines on campus bore a strange but impeccable resemblance to him. He was better known as the main "stud" by the employees of the college who watched him grow from kittenhood. He was also known for his position in the cat hierarchy and all the others would step aside when he sat down for dinner. Some of the people would get annoyed with him because his dining manners were appalling and he was known to push even the tiniest kitten away from the food in deference to himself.

As a social worker and the purveyor of impossible tasks, I became intrigued with the idea of rescuing this infamous cat character. So I began, in the winter of 1991 – February to be exact to pursue and hopefully trap this monument of the Ramapo College feral cat world. (I, of course, was on the mission of trapping and placing all the cats on the campus at that time.) My associate and private in the army of two, Michael, would reluctantly meet me every evening on campus for the nightly ritual of trying to catch Moby Dick. His name became apparent after the first few months of failure. Michael and I both have advanced degrees but neither of us with ingenuity and creativity could snag our boy. If there was another cat in the area, Moby would communicate the danger and sometimes even prevent our plan for capture. For months, this protocol would be followed nightly but no success was had. We created a trap with a fake mouse which dangled from a man-operated string so that it would move when he was in view. He snubbed his nose at that trick. We tranquilized him under the direction of a veterinarian and invited the animal control officer up to assist us while Moby was under the influence. That plan, too, was aborted by Moby. As spring became summer and summer fall, our frustration heightened. Again, as a social worker, I networked to find the experts in "cat rescue." I succeeded but my efforts were to no avail because Moby was smarter than all of us. In the interim, I celebrated holidays with Moby by bringing him turkey on Thanksgiving and fish on Christmas Eve. On the day before New Year's Eve with Michael's new hand made trap, some catnip, and my homemade meatloaf our mission was completed. Moby went into the trap. What euphoria we felt that night. He was the last stray on the campus at that time and we had succeeded in our efforts to denude Ramapo College of their cat population.

The next episode in Moby's life began with what to do with him. As his gray steely eyes pierced me through the large cage which he inhabited for three months, I remained ambivalent. Do I move him to my cat sanctuary in my home or do I release him to the organization which retrains feral cats and looks toward adoption? You guessed it. He spent the next seven years romping with the other cats in my home and retaining his position in the hierarchy as the "king" of the cats. He also became the king of my bed, my pillow, and my heart and toward the end of our relationship took the spot on my pillow at night where my head should rest. Each morning he would get up and expect to be the first one petted. No one dared to usurp his place. His eyes got softer and he was my constant companion. I achieved what I had set out to do. That was, to form a bond, close and unconditional, with this majestic beast who was thought not to be domesticated.

Moby did his job as my companion but more than that he showed me that impossible dreams do come true and what's more feral cats can be domesticated. In the last week of his life, he was looking for a place to die. He searched the house through. I made every effort to keep him from his journey including preparing for him his most beloved meatloaf. He was quite excited by it at first but then looked up and communicated to me that not even the meatloaf could divert him from his journey. He passed in the vet's office on that fateful Friday in February. We had come full circle to meet in February and depart from each other in February as well. He looked at me as if to say "Good-Bye Mommy." He then rested his face on my hand, the hand which so often had been raised to pet and comfort him and with gratitude and love he left my life. His love will never be forgotten.

In today's society, where a strong extended family is less common and there are more single parent homes than ever before, and in an economic climate where both parents are employed outside of the home, the importance of a family pet in the home seems to be gaining significance especially with children. Our attachment to our pets and the grief experienced as a result of the death of those pets are issues which impact on people of all ages. An understanding of the nature and substance of children's responses to the loss of their pet and the depth of the feelings experienced is essential in helping them cope with their loss. Anticipated or sudden death and its impact on children are areas of concern for parents and professionals.

Most information which has been written to date does not deal specifically with children and loss. This book deals with children's response to loss at different ages in children's lives. Some have done research dealing with adults' response to loss and others have been involved with the positive relationship of people and their pets as well as the intensity of grief experienced after a loss. All of these endeavors have been the result of information gathered about adults and by adults. I examined children's attachment and the duration and level of grief in response to loss over a one-year period in a recent research project. Some write that the human grief process for companion animals is deep, painful and sometimes exceeds the bounds of human loss. The relationship between pet and owner is usually less ambivalent than with humans and we find more sadness than anger. Through the steps of grief as we know them, people who lose pets usually don't experience anger toward their lost pet. The resolution of grief is unpredictable and often surpasses the length of time seen with human loss. It is an individual response and so it must be treated considering the uniqueness of each person. "Disenfranchised grief" and the need for our society to give credibility to losses outside of one's traditional family constellation should be considered in the case of pet loss. It is often hard for us to share our grief with the people around us as they sometimes diminish its importance. The result is isolation for the pet owner.

What is bereavement and grief?

Let me start with the definition of bereavement. It is defined as the "total response pattern, psychological and physiological, displayed by an individual following the loss of a significant object, usually a loved one" (Averill 1968, p.721). Grief is only one component of bereavement. It is an emotional suffering caused by death or bereavement. Grief involves a sequence of thoughts and feelings that follow the loss and accompanying mourning. Grief is a process, and as a result is not a specific emotion like fear or sadness but instead is a group of feelings that can be expressed by many thoughts, emotions, and behaviors. Grief is the internal meaning given to the external event. The normal grief responses seem to include "somatic distress (such as headaches, upset stomach, flushing, etc.), guilt, anger, preoccupation with the image of the deceased, and agitated, non-goal directed behavior" (Lindemann, cited in Brasted and Callahan 1984, p.530). The pets identified by most people through my counseling experience have been domesticated cats, dogs, birds, hamsters, guinea pigs, gerbils or any other animals which are kept for pleasure and enjoyment as opposed to working animals.

Can one grieve without attachment?

The questions which I have examined through my experiences are as follows: How does human attachment work at different stages of life? Does the length of the grief period after a significant loss vary at different times in a person's existence? Does the quality of grief change if the loss was anticipated as opposed to a sudden loss?

Many researchers dealing with child behavior and development support the idea that attachment occurs outside of the animal drives for food and sex. They offer as the basis of attachment the need for "safety" and "security." The parent or a close adult who understands the child's need for comfort and protection and at the same time permits the child's need for independent investigation of the environment will help the child to grow as an esteemed and self-assured adult.

It most often takes attachment to a person or pet to grieve their loss. The closer the attachment is, the greater the grief response. Some say that affective life is blended with the intellect, that is, you can't love if you don't understand. The assumption is that the child's attachment comes as a result of having his or her needs fulfilled. In terms of grief, the process of grief in children can be observed from as early as the age of 12 months. The mourning process includes the "unconscious yearning" for the lost being; "unconscious reproach" which includes anger at the person or being for leaving; "compulsive" caregiving which includes always trying to help others when deep inside you want the care and help yourself; and the feeling that the loss cannot be permanent. On the other hand, some specialists speak of grief focusing on the individual's ability to understand the irreversibility and finality of death. The person shows moral concern and empathy outside of him or herself. These specialists say that this begins to happen during early adolescence.

How can I tell if my child is attached to our pet?
In order for children to mourn for the loss of their pets, there must first be an attachment. This is an essential component of grief no matter what the age of the person. Four areas for attachment of children to their pets are as follows:

1. How much time and activity does the child devote to the pet?

2. How much attention and affection does the child give to the pet?

3. How well does the child know the companion animal?

4. How does the child behave toward the pet?

It is important also to assess the amount of time and quality of activities the child shares with his or her pet. It is essential that questions that pertain to the four areas are asked as well as observing the child with the pet. There are three types of attachment: affective, cognitive and behavioral. These areas are defined as intimacy, thoughts about the pet and time spent on those thoughts, and the actual caring for the pet. As the child gets older these areas develop. That is, their feelings of intimacy with the pet, their time spent with the pet, as well as thoughts and talk about the pet with friends and family, and their real involvement with the caretaking of the pet are more important. Duties such as feeding, watering, walking the dog, cleaning litter or cages are more realistic obligations of the child. Accompanying parents to the veterinarian with a sick pet also becomes more feasible. All of the above activities add to the child's attachment to the pet and their ability to develop emotional ties. Because of the unconditional love which is given by the pet, a very deep and fulfilling relationship often develops between the child and the pet.

These principles of attachment could even be applied in the case of very young children. The feelings involved in the intimacy and time spent with a pet seem to be of greater duration during a child's early years. Through my experience, children between the ages of six and ten who were interviewed had intensive grief after the loss of their pet. They experienced somatic symptoms such as headaches and stomach aches after their pet died. They cried often, were angry about their loss, had a strong wish to have their pet back, and felt particularly sad at times during the day when they used to play with their pet. Some wrote letters to their pet and expressed their sadness and loneliness at specific times during the day when they missed their pet the most. They also expressed their feelings through drawings or poetry. The subject of concern was often where the pet was now such as, in heaven, or what the child remembered doing with his or her pet.

What is anticipatory grief?

"Anticipatory grief" is explained as knowing that the love object is going to die before the actual death occurs. In this type of grief a person experiences the grief response similar to that of normal grief but before the actual death. These grievers have a shortened grief reaction after the actual death occurs. It has been shown that young children grieved more than adults after the loss of their pet even if the grief was anticipated.

Anticipated grief is a much more complicated set of circumstances. There are many scenarios faced by families dealing with these phenomena. In my work with grieving patients it was noted that anticipatory grief for all ages seems to lessen the effect of grief when the pet actually dies. A pet may be facing euthanasia because of a terminal illness or old age, as well as experiencing behavioral problems. It may have been diagnosed with a terminal illness with a definite time-limited expectation to its life. A family may be moving to another home where their pet is not permitted. These as well as other contingencies may be the situation. A basic rule of thumb is to discuss the problem openly in a family forum. Each family member should be granted the true expression of his or her feelings. Each person should be sensitive to the position of the other family members. When the decision is imminent, it should truly be the judgment of the adult head(s) of the family when and if the event should occur. Children, especially prior to late adolescence, cannot assume the responsibility of such a decision. It would be as if a parent gave the car keys to a child and asked him or her to drive, without a license and training to be proficient at the skill. Too many times, parents defer these decisions to children who are later left with unresolved guilt. I once was called for a consultation with a family whose pet was old and infirm but not diseased. He could no longer walk and was incontinent. The family was quite conflicted about what to do. Each had his or her own set of values and experiences with the dog. Each member of the family spoke and defined his or her position. In the end, the parents made the very difficult decision to have the pet euthanized. The event took place in the home where all the family could support the pet and each other. I knew another family with teenagers who spent a lot of time grieving their loss and talking about how it would be when Sam died. He was an old dog having severe muscle and motor problems. They cried and talked about what life would be like when he was gone. The next day he was euthanized and they reported a sense of relief and felt they were sad but the feelings were not as intense as before his death.

Anticipated grief is often referred to as a time for rehearsal. It permits the opportunity for review of the pet's life with the child as well as what life will be like when that member of the family is gone. Children who can understand the basic game of "peek-a-boo" can understand the concept of the final disappearance of a person or pet. This early childhood game is one where a child covers his or her eyes and the object that he or she was looking at disappears. It is used to understand the notion of the disappearance of the attachment object. When a child is verbal, a parent can talk about the fact that our pet cannot live anymore and needs to go to rest or pass away or die. The more often a parent can use the actual word "die" the more comfortable the child will be with the reality. A parent can discuss the process of euthanasia as a humane method of allowing the pet to expire. The process can be explained in a direct, non-judgmental way. For

example, a young boy at the age of six was brought to my
office after his family dog was euthanized. His mother
was quite concerned about the child because he obsessed
about the dog's death and wondered why he wasn't told
before the event occurred. He felt betrayed by his parents
as well as by the veterinarian, whom he had visited many
times before this incident took place. He felt a loss of trust
with the adults in his environment. He was an
exceptionally bright boy who could articulate his
feelings. He was both angry and sad. When in the session
his mother realized the impact of the event she was able to
communicate with the child and express her feelings
openly to him. He needed two sessions to resolve his
problems but I'm sure that the sadness he felt lasted a
much longer period of time.

Does the child understand what death really is?
The controversy about a child's understanding of death
and the feelings that follow is disputed by many writers
on the subject. My position supports the concept that the
child understands that death is not reversible and that it is
expected that one feels sad at the loss (death) of a close
person or companion animal. In my experience even
children at age four understand that "Fluffy" is not coming
back home. Even if the child is very young and does not
understand that death is permanent, he or she still feels the
emptiness and loss of the loved one who they miss.
Children, when given a supportive and trusting environment to support their feelings, will allow those feelings to
surface and communicate them to those very close to

them. These conclusions have been seen in practice over the years.

Parents may think that since a child is not showing a reaction to the death of a pet or a loved one, he or she is not understanding or not reacting to that loss. It may be that the child does not know how to verbalize the feelings or ask the pertinent questions to clarify his or her emotional reaction. The child may still be in the stage of shock and not yet able to express his or her emotions. A parent once told me a story of how her child was too frightened to sleep after the family dog was euthanized. Let's face it, children think in concrete and literal terms. The six-year-old little girl was told that the dog went to "heaven" after the veterinarian put the animal to "sleep". When the parent understood that the child's fears surrounded the dog's disappearance after it went to sleep, the parent then explained to the child the reality of the death. The parent also clarified that a person or a pet does not die when they go to sleep. After this explanation, the child began to sleep well again.

When is professional help needed?

Sometimes children begin to withdraw from daily activities for periods of time (a week or two is normal). They might not want to attend school anymore and become very clingy. They may obsess about death and fear that they too will die. Each person has his or her individual time span to grieve but when their daily normal functioning is impeded it is time to seek some help.

In cases where professional help is needed after the loss, a counselor needs to clarify and understand the problems which might underpin a person's depression. If a person is experiencing unresolved mourning or grief that involves the loss of a companion animal and that person is ashamed of his or her feelings, it is important that those feelings are validated. A practitioner, who is aware that grief and bereavement for a deceased pet exists, and research supports this premise, would be better able to assist the person through the grieving process. If that person is a child, the professional needs to clue the parent or guardian in so that they too understand the depth and severity of the loss and ways to help their child cope.

Are adolescents' responses different from those of younger children?

Adolescents have a particularly hard time expressing their feelings about the attachment and grief that they experience after losing a pet. It is a stage of immortality where these children feel that they and those around them are invincible. I'm speaking of children between the ages of 13 and 17 years old. At this stage of development when they are experimenting with values and feelings of independence, it is extremely hard to face the intimate feelings experienced toward the family pet. They often tend to minimize the loss and feel that it's not "cool" to grieve. Yet, when asked how they felt after the loss they too experienced sadness and anger. They find themselves talking to pictures of their lost pet, looking for the pet as they walk down the street and even experience themselves dreaming of their pet when it was alive. Emily used to spend time after a date reviewing the details of the evening with her pet beagle, Barney, and she swore he understood her. But after his death she found those moments after arriving home from a date most painful because she acutely experienced his loss at that time.

Another very difficult time in adolescence is when the family pet dies when the teen goes off to college. If a family is to get a pet, it usually occurs when the child is between the ages of six and nine years old. Since the average life span for a dog is about ten years this would put the pet's death at about the time when the youngster would be at college. Should parents tell the adolescent about the loss or should that person have input as part of the family as to the euthanizing of the pet and the arrangements for disposal? These are important questions to be dealt with in each family. It seems to be a natural instinct of parents to protect their children from the experience of death. Often parents avoid telling their children (who are away at school) of any adversity that may befall the family. Their children can very often sense the distress and feel isolated and left out of the family rhythm because they have not been told. Bobbie was away at an Ivy League college during his freshman year. His mother reminded him to say "good-bye" to his old dog "Freddie" each time Bobbie left home to return to school after a break. His dog was 15 years old when the young man began college. One Sunday afternoon in early April his dog laid down and died. His mother, in an effort to protect her son, didn't tell him of the death until he came home from school for the summer. When the boy discovered his dog was dead he mourned throughout the summer but in my office confided that he felt a sense of alienation that his parents did not share the experience of the loss with him at the time it occurred. His mother, on the other hand, felt she needed to protect her son especially while he was adjusting to college. It is a difficult call but I would err on the side of disclosure because even an eruptive reaction would help the young person still feel a part of his family system and included in its function.

Is the grieving process different for sudden or accidental deaths?

In cases where the pet is killed accidentally or dies suddenly as the result of a hospital procedure, the grief is extremely intense during the first few days. It appears that an immediate response is often quite difficult because the person is in shock. There is often heightened guilt when such an event takes place. A young veterinarian came to my office grief and guilt stricken when her dog died during a routine surgery. She blamed herself for not seeing the signs of the serious illness before the operation and then could not comprehend what life would be like for herself without her close companion. On another occasion, I was in the veterinarian's office awaiting treatment for one of my pets. I overheard the receptionist telling a seven-year-old child that it was not an emergency because a squirrel had just been hit by a car in front of her home. The child was distraught and suggested to the technician that she call "911." In this case the child was responding with sensitivity to an animal's pain even though it was not her animal. It is very hard to explain and difficult for each child to understand that we don't provide the same type of concern or services for wild animals as we do for our own animals or for humans. As you can see, the child at the age of seven reacted to the squirrel's accident with the same care and concern she would have expressed for her own pet. The way our society has of deciding who receives and does not receive medical attention is difficult for a child to understand. It is sophisticated and, at times, unexplainable. When you consider it as an adult it is also difficult to comprehend yet we have a hierarchy of whom we care for and whom we ignore.

How can we explain euthanasia to children?

In cases where aggressive pet behavior is the cause of the impending death, it is more difficult for parents to explain this decision to their child. A very young child should be carefully told of this decision. They might interpret that the reason for death is poor behavior and if this can happen to my pet why not me? The child should be told of the dangers of having a pet that is not tame. It is essential that parents explore every other contingency before making this final decision. One cannot be sure of a child's interpretation of the event since children reach their own conclusions about such events and adults do not always find these easy to discern. In such situations it becomes tempting to tell the child a prevarication. Often, children sense such stories are untrue and trust can erode in the relationship. With older children, it is always best to be straightforward. Parents sometimes take the path of least resistance when dealing with their child and tell them a lie about the fate of the pet but eventually resentment can emerge as a result of this type of deception. The issues of anger and sadness toward the pet emerge since the child perceives that it was the pet's choice to misbehave and therefore to terminate the relationship.

It is difficult for all of us not to attribute human characteristics and parameters to a pet's behavior. Bernard, a lovely shar-pei, was from a prize winning line. The family brought a rabbit into the home and tried to socialize the dog with the rabbit. When the dog became friendly with the rabbit and comfortable in his presence, everyone in the family relaxed about the two pets getting along. Contrary to the dog's behavior in the home, when he saw the rabbit in the backyard, Bernard attacked and killed it in front of the children. Jerry, the ten-year-old boy in the family, was traumatized by this event because of its unpredictability and the absolute horror that he witnessed. One cannot be sure of a pet's behavior in different environments. The rabbit was prey to the dog when seen in an outside environment. This occurrence must be explained to the children in very simple terms and they should be allowed to express their anger and feelings of dismay in the safety of their home.

Billy, a rather large four-year-old, came to see me after biting a boy in nursery school. The boy had harassed Billy. When asked why he used biting as a form of aggression Billy explained that he had seen his dog do that.

How long does grief normally last?

"Normal" grief is an individual response. It has been found that not only is age an issue but the time that has elapsed since the death of the pet is also of concern. The overall consensus observed in each age category is that grief is worse during the one- to four-month interval after the death of the pet. It has also been noted that grief experienced by those who lost their pets five months ago is very similar to those who lost their pets 12 months ago. Again, the most significant grief is usually experienced during the first four months after the loss of a pet no matter what the cause of death or how much a person anticipated the loss. It is interesting to find that there are very few people of any age who can even speak about the loss during the first week after the experience. The veterinarians I contacted felt that those clients who had just lost a pet could not even be approached to talk to a professional about the event because they were too grief-ridden. It took at least two weeks before they could be asked. If the parents didn't want to speak, you could be sure that they would not permit their children to do so. As we know, parents are very protective of their children and feel it necessary to shield them from even the thought of the loss as if thinking about it would cause them more difficulties. When a loss occurs one of the most important aspects of grief relief is talking about the event and sharing the feelings.

Chapter 2

Signs and Symptoms
of Grief in Children

Reflection: **A Sudden Death and Longstanding Grief**
Michael Ardizzone

Jordan was a big cat, about 24 lbs, but he wasn't obese like most cats of that weight. He was just a big-boned, large cat. A little too fat, yes. Too sedentary, yes. But he wasn't so fat that I expected him to die of a heart attack at age six-and-a-half.

I knew Jordan almost his entire life. My friend Joanne and I caught Jordan and his brother Dutch as ten-week-old kittens on the campus of Ramapo College in New Jersey. We used to rescue strays there, and during one nighttime patrol, we saw the two kittens under the book return outside the library. We had only two have-a-heart traps and we had set both of them for other kittens on campus that we were trying to catch. Without a trap, we decided to lure the kittens into a carrier and then close the door on them. It seemed like Mission Impossible: catch two large kittens in a carrier at the same time without spooking them.

We put food in the carrier and waited. Once they were inside eating, I snuck up behind the carrier, barefoot so I wouldn't make any noise. But since I was behind the carrier, and couldn't see the front to determine if the cats were entirely inside, Joanne – standing 50 yards away – had to motion to me with her hands to let me know when to approach the carrier and shut the door. We had to be absolutely silent or the kittens would spook and dart out of the carrier.

Well, it worked, and Mr. Phelps would have been proud of how we coordinated the mission. Employing the quickest reflexes I could muster, I closed the door of the carrier in an instant and we caught both kittens.

Less than a year prior, I had a dream about having a blue cat. So when I saw Jordan, who was almost entirely blue except for a white "bow tie," I immediately started to rationalize arguments for keeping him. And of course since I didn't want to split up the kittens I would have to keep the other kitten too. His brother Dutch was a grey tiger, smaller and more skittish than Jordan.

After watching Jordan grow up, and taking care of him for almost his entire life, it was hard to lose him without any warning. I had weathered the loss of too many family members, but almost always there was a warning, an illness. Death visited Jordan without a clue.

One night on my way home from work, something told me to go straight home. I needed to stop at the store, for cat food of all things, but something told me not to. When I arrived home, and went downstairs to feed the cats, I found out what it was.

The second I descended the stairs, I saw Jordan, lying still in his cat bed, and I knew something was wrong. Even when your cat is sleeping and perfectly still, you sense movement, you sense life. But there's an abrupt stillness about death. And sure enough, Jordan was dead.

My intuition tried to warn me. A few days before his death, something made me hold Jordan in my arms. He usually didn't like to be held; like many cats who were wild as kittens, he remained a little wary of humans all his life. But this time, he stayed in my arms and seemed comfortable.

I was frustrated that I wasn't there with him at the end. I probably couldn't have done anything, but I might have been able to alleviate his fear in the last moments of his life. I thought of my dog of 14 years, Butch; I wasn't there when he died either. He left his body in the cold, impersonal kennel at the vet's office, missing I'm sure, the boy with whom he grew up and shared his life. And the thought of him leaving this life alone, without me there, has bothered me ever since.

The death of my dog Butch wasn't the first feeling of regret that I carried from childhood. My mother's family owned what used to be considered a junkyard – today it would be called a recycling center – and they had dogs to guard the premises. When I was about four, my parents brought home one of the dogs, a white German shepherd named Winnie. It seems that I was allergic (probably to something else, but it was blamed on Winnie) and so Winnie went back to the junkyard with the rest of the dogs. A few years later, there was a fire there and Winnie, a beautiful dog with a sweet disposition, was never seen again, presumed dead. I was crushed. I felt responsible for her death. And in the same way that Charles Foster Kane of *Citizen Kane* longed all his life for his boyhood sled Rosebud, I have longed to make things right and give a better life to a white German shepherd.

> The loss of each of my animal friends has been tough for me. I think one of the reasons I'm an "animal person" is because I can get closer to them than I can to people. Another cat of mine, Jane, was with me for 19 years. At the time of her death, her friendship was the oldest in my life. Perhaps I can get closer to pets because they are never sarcastic or hateful – characteristics of all too many people. No, pets offer a safe emotional haven. And when death invades that haven, it leaves a permanent void.

What are the signs and symptoms of grief in children?

Throughout my experience, I have found that children do exhibit the same feelings as adults after a loss but that children do not always show the outward signs and are thus looked upon as not understanding or not feeling the loss. Children do feel the loss but are reluctant to share the feelings unless in a safe environment (Raphael 1983). This response is sometimes different from that of an adult and too often children's reactions are either compared to adults or neglected as not existing since they are not recognized by the adult community. Glen, a six-year-old boy, was harboring feelings of guilt because he was the family member who opened the door when the family dog ran out into the street and was killed by an automobile. Neither his parents nor his other siblings had known that this child felt fully responsible for the death of the family pet. He had been experiencing anger at school but after the disclosure was able to mourn and assume his prior state of equilibrium.

Should adults shield children from death?

Adults sometimes shield children from death. The parent thinks that if you don't share the death with the child, they will not know about it. Ironically, children will not always let their parents know that they are aware of the death because in some ways the children are protecting their parents. Children often find themselves protecting their parents. They are unconditionally loyal and their love for their parent prevents them from showing how much pain they are really feeling. Children are new to the expressions of grief and unless they have role models to help them to express their feelings appropriately they often just let them fester inside. Monica was an 18-year-old girl who was in pathological mourning. She exhibited a malaise that could not be attributed to any known cause. After months of treatment, I discovered that the loss of her dog when she was ten years old was still causing her untold grief. At that time, the family decided to give their dog away since it was too big and unwieldy. The dog, a German shepherd, had been given to a guard dog company. He was trained and held "hostage" during the day and at night was made to patrol a car dealership. After Monica had spent months worrying about him, her parents admitted that he had been killed while jumping off the truck on the way to his placement. As she told the story eight years later, she wept with such deep sorrow as though it had just occurred. She believed that he was trying to find his way back home because he missed her. We dealt with that loss for weeks and amazingly the depression began to lift. I was convinced that the loss which had occurred so many years before was responsible for the reactive depression that she exhibited.

Death should be looked at as a normal process at the end of life. If we take the taboo away from death and speak of it openly it will be less foreboding. The basic problem is that we are not comfortable with speaking about it so we don't. This lack of communication about the dying process causes children to fear it and deny that it exists. When it occurs we are shocked and dismayed but again regain our mechanism of denial so that it is never fully dealt with. Speaking about death calmly and sharing our feelings of sadness and grief with children even though uncomfortable gives them comfort and safety. As long as we provide a model for our children, they will feel safe and will be able to handle anything.

Should we deny that grief exists after the loss of a pet?

Our society is deeply committed to denying that children experience grief. We often say that if the child doesn't have a cognitive understanding of death then he or she cannot experience the feelings of grief. Parents, in particular, hold to their denial since it is difficult for them to conceive of their children as suffering the pangs of grief. None of us want to see our children in pain, emotional or otherwise. It becomes easier to deny that such pain exists. Often parents are so preoccupied dealing with their own sorrow that it is more convenient to deny the child's feelings. How much more the pain would be if we accepted the fact that our children were feeling as badly as we were or in many cases even worse. Alice, a ten-year-old girl, had just lost her family pet. When sitting in the session with her mother, she would watch her mother out of the corner of her eye to see if her mother was going to cry. If the mother began to cry the youngster would try to tell a joke or change the subject. The mother had brought the child in for therapy but it was obvious that the mother was overwhelmed with grief. When I met with the child on her own, she admitted how she tried to cheer her mother up because she was so upset over the loss. When in session alone, the child was able to deal with her own grief and ask important questions about death that she did not feel comfortable asking in front of her mother.

How is grief experienced by children aged one to three?

Grief is seen in very young children (infancy–preschool, one to three years old) with bouts of crying and longing for the lost attachment figure. They may roam around the house looking for the dead pet or even call out to him or her. They don't understand the concept of death but that doesn't mean that they don't feel the pangs of the loss. A member of the family is missing and they are distressed and long for the return of the pet.

What to do

Spend time with the child. Validate his or her feelings and allow them to show their feelings when they come. We have a tendency to try and stop children from crying and being sad. Tell them that it is OK to be sad because that is the feeling they are experiencing. Our modeling of appropriate behavior is helpful to them. They should be made to feel comfortable with their feelings: the negative as well as the positive. Let the child know that the pet is no longer available but that you are there with them to support and help work through their feelings. Hugging and comforting is quite appropriate at this time.

How is grief experienced by children aged four to six?

In the pre and early elementary school years (four to six years old), children understand that the pet has gone to a place where they can no longer be together. They become distressed but they usually have verbal skills that younger children do not. That is, they can express their sadness about not seeing the pet or feeling the warmth of the pet being close to them. The rituals that they may have adopted with the pet, such as playing ball, feeding or possibly sleeping with the pet are no longer done. This condition prompts a great deal of loneliness and bewilderment. They are often told that the pet went to heaven but have no concept of where or what heaven is. They may feel responsible for the pet's disappearance since they may have been impatient or angry with the pet before it was lost. If the loss was not anticipated and the child in this age group was not prepared for the pet's passing, the child may be in a state of shock. That is, a sense of numbness overcomes him or her until the pain of emotional loss can be dealt with. If children are not handled carefully during this age period they may begin to withdraw and feel more comfortable staying at home. They may not feel the security necessary to know that no one else in the family is going to leave or die when they are at school. They also begin to fear the death of other pets or even family members or themselves. Children at this age level don't know what causes death so they may question their own mortality. Oftentimes, children do not communicate these concerns but rather hold them inside. Possibly, they don't know how to verbalize these concerns or through magical thinking are afraid if they utter them they can cause them to occur. Their sense of security may be shaken and they need to be told that their parent will protect them and provide a safe environment. This is essential to the resolution of grief at this stage of development.

What to do

Allow the child to speak of the pet and remember the special times they had together. You cannot nag children into experiencing the pain but you can gently suggest how you are feeling and that if they have similar feelings they can share them. You might ask them to draw a picture of the pet as they remember them or as they were dying or even depicting where they are now. Recently I had a young child of six years in my office. Vicki was involved in sand play therapy and wanted to bury every figure in the sand. We then focused on her cat who had died about a year ago and I asked if she wanted to draw Jimmy. She drew him with a smile playing with her (also smiling) in the yard as the sun shone over them.

How is grief experienced by children aged seven to nine?

The next age group, seven to nine-year-olds, do understand that death is final. These are children who see the world as a safe and secure place. They look up to their parents and teachers. They enjoy play, friends and school. Their world is ideal and they feel protected and comfortable in it. When they experience the loss of a pet, it can be traumatic. One of the first signs of grief in this group is withdrawal from activities. They may withdraw or misbehave in school. They may talk about and obsess about death. It may intrude into their fantasy play or may appear in acts of aggression toward friends. Children in this age group may also become extremely attached or dependent on their parents. Often, the grief expressed during this age period is delayed since it is hard for children to deal with the pain involved in the mourning process. Mikey exhibited a great deal of impulsive behavior. During one session he told me that he had lost his dog during the prior week. He chose to tell me about it as he left my office. The next week I asked about the dog's death and he said that he chose not to discuss the matter. He explained that boys don't cry. The following week I prepared a printout of Paul C. Dahm's poem "Rainbow Bridge" (Dahm 1998) and asked him to read it with me. He broke down and cried and the following week sat on his mother's lap and cried with grief and deep sadness. This youngster expressed his sadness and loss through aggressive behavior toward peers and siblings. After he began to deal with his feelings, these explosive events began to dissipate.

What to do

A family service commemorating the pet's life and death with all the family present would be appropriate. Children like family occasions and also want to know that the adults are in control. A keepsake box of pictures or maybe even the pet's license or collar might be put in the box as well as a "good-bye" letter that the child could write to the pet.

How do 10 to 12-year-old children express their grief?

The next age group, 10 to 12-year-olds, are basically pre-adolescent. They hang together in same-sex groups and still enjoy school, play and friends. During this period children know that death is inevitable. They realize that all living creatures have to die. When the loss of a pet occurs during this time the child is grief stricken and mourning is similar to that of the adult. Death is understood but is accepted as a normal event in the life cycle. It is difficult for children in this age group to accept death as occurring in young people or young pets. It is what happens to old people and old pets. Josie was 11 years old when her favorite cat, Rolly, died. He was two years old. Her sensitivity was acute as was her deep sorrow over the loss of this cat, her companion. He was too young to die and to die so suddenly. She mourned for months and felt as if her child had died. At times, she was inconsolable. She knew she would never see or touch him again and that loss was uniquely unbearable. At the same time her grandmother was dying. She accepted that more readily since she was an old person who lived far away.

What to do

At this age a ceremony is still effective. Talking about death as part of the life process and sharing your own feelings with the child is still appropriate. Letting the child decide who to invite to the ceremony and maybe participating in it would also be fitting. At this stage a child is old enough and it is helpful for them to join their parents in the plans for the commemoration.

How do adolescents experience grief?

Adolescence, a period of omnipotence and independence, is characterized by cavalier behavior. The rest of my family members are "freaks" but not me. I'm different. There is denial of sadness and pain which is a typical defense against reality. Adolescents are just beginning their adult existence and want to imitate what adults would do or at least what they think adults would do. They prefer to deny vulnerability which is part of the grieving process. Many times, their grief is inhibited until a time when they can no longer deny it and usually explode at some other event when in fact it is the loss of their pet that they are upset about. Mitchell was suspended from school for calling his teacher a "jerk." When his parents were called they told the principal that their 13-year-old labrador had died the night before. Mitch had not even blinked when told of the loss and made fun of his sister for crying.

The loss of a companion animal during this period brings the young person "up short" and sometimes propels him or her into adulthood because of the crisis and grief experienced. Loss of a loved one at this stage appears to be a "rite of passage."

What to do

During this stage, it is hard to predict the response of the teen. Denial or acting out may be the expression of grief. Offer to have the young person talk to you and share your feelings and emotional response openly. They eventually will mourn the loss but in their own time and way. Always remember that an adolescent is sometimes a young child in a "big" body.

Chapter 3

The Grief Process
in Children

Reflection: **For the Love of Looie**
Arthur Chill

Many years ago a lady in my payroll department named
Marilyn used to feed this tiny, feral calico cat she named
Kahlua. She had litter after litter and it was amazing that she
survived, especially the winters. After her last litter, I thought
it was time that I did something about it. I was determined
to rescue her and give her a home. With much perseverance
and luck, I successfully trapped her and her litter. They [the
kittens] were so adorable. I easily found homes for them.
Before introducing her into my home with the other cats, I
had her tested, inoculated, and spayed. I renamed her Looie
(the name I called her in the wild). She eventually became
trusting and loving and we became great friends. She loved
to be scratched and brushed as she lounged on a plush chair.
(A far cry from the bushes and rock wall she formerly lived
in.) After about 12 years with us, she developed a thyroid
condition and we would give her medication twice a day.
She was reduced to only six pounds. After about six months
of treatment, one morning I went in to feed her and her

breathing was labored and she couldn't walk without falling over. We rushed her to the vet and he felt a mass in her stomach. The difficult decision to let her go was an emotional but easy choice when it would spare her suffering any longer. I greatly miss my good friend but I have the memories of 12 years of a dear, sweet (once wild) kitty that would have suffered in the wild and would have died an agonizing death a long time ago if I didn't make the effort to give her a better life.

Can we assign a prescribed period of grief and mourning?

The phenomenon of grief is often misunderstood. Grief is the personal experience of loss. Mourning is the process that is gone through by the bereft individual. As we, in our society, become more and more efficient and conscious of expediting tasks, mourning and the grief that ensues becomes an intolerant event especially if it is prolonged. We assign an imaginary time to the length one should grieve for a lost love. When I worked at a local high school, the personal bereavement leave permitted for a death was as follows: for a parent – three days; for a child – a week; for a spouse – a week. There was never a time allowed for the loss of a companion animal. When staff returned from a bereavement leave, it was expected that they would be emotionally the same as before the loss and would not show any signs of emotion. Most people complied with that requirement not that they did not feel the pangs of grief underneath the facade. In the past, our European predecessors during their assigned time of mourning would spend one year dressed in black garb and the second year of mourning dressed in black and white. Was this time allotment more accurate? It might have been prolonged but it at least allowed the participant enough time to experience the feelings that ensued after a significant loss.

Does everyone go through the mourning process after a loss?

After a loss, each of us copes in a particular way. Depending upon the attachment to the lost figure, the personal experience of grief does vary. Danny came to my office after his dog, Shannon, was euthanized. He was seemingly mildly affected by the loss. The dog was 18 years old and Danny was six. Danny didn't remember ever playing with Shannon as she was old when he arrived and most children don't remember events before the age of three. In this case, we see a lack of attachment to the companion animal and so the mourning process is not significant. Danny may think he needs to be sad to emulate his parents' feelings. In another case, Jane (age ten) was notably attached to her cat, Pumpkin. He had been with her since age four. Jane was a shy child who didn't go out and play much and really had few friends. She spent much of her spare time with Pumpkin talking to him and taking care of his needs. When he died suddenly of heart failure, she was despondent. Her parents did not understand her feelings and her father thought she was psychologically ill. Jane was isolated and alone in her grief and had no one to share it with. As I explained, not everyone goes through the grief process to the same extent. The degree of attachment to the lost figure really determines the depth of the grief and length of the mourning process.

What are some of the normal grief reactions observed in grieving children?

Children go through some of the same feelings as adults. The mourning process and grief related to it can be seen expressed as emotions of sadness, anger, shock, yearning, numbness, a sense of relief, guilt and anxiety. The physical symptoms are also experienced by children. These may include but are not confined to: tightening of the muscles in the throat and chest; sinking feeling in the stomach; butterflies; hollow feelings in the chest and stomach; headache; tension in the muscles; lack of physical energy; rapid heart beat and feeling as though they can't catch their breathe; the inability to eat; and the inability to sleep or sleeping too much. Some of the cognitive reactions may include but are not limited to: yearning for the lost object; seeing the lost object or feeling his or her presence; and difficulty concentrating or having many thoughts intruding his or her countenance.

Children experience sadness in particular after the loss of a pet. It can be felt as a nagging emptiness inside the person or a pervasive feeling of anguish. Some of the adjectives that describe this feeling in children might be gloomy, heavy-hearted, melancholy, and heart-broken. That love object that was there unconditionally is now absent. The absence of the after school playmate who was so happy to see them when they returned from school leaves an empty void in the child's world. Many children called "latchkey kids" return home from school with no one to greet them but their pet. Seth was a ten-year-old boy who found himself in trouble quite often in school. His mother was a school teacher who didn't return home until at least an hour after he came home from school. He was greeted with excitement and kisses from his dog, Edgar, each afternoon. When Edgar died, Seth was saddened beyond his ability to express himself. At first, he seemed numb but then he cried and felt guilty thinking that his poor behavior in school was punished by Edgar's death. He told his mother that he saw Edgar's footprints in the hall carpet and heard his bark when he began to open the door when he came home from school. Was Seth becoming psychotic? No, he was just a child responding to his grief reaction with both feelings and cognitive responses.

Another feeling seen in children but less when a pet is lost than when a person is lost is anger. It is an irrational feeling response related to grief. Most often this anger is about the significant other leaving and the idea of the loneliness that the loss creates. Because it is an irrational feeling, it is hard for us to come to terms with. How can we possibly be angry with Fido; he didn't mean to die. The feeling that follows this one is guilt. The child or person who has lost the pet feels guilty for feeling angry toward the deceased. Guilt is also seen as an irrational response of children. For example, Margaret was guilt ridden because before her cat ran away from home she told Susie, "Get lost, you're annoying me with your licking." Margaret felt that her words caused her cat to run away. Several days later the cat was found dead. She was killed by a car.

The sudden death, which I just referred to, can elicit feelings of shock and numbness in children. The shock of a sudden death leads to feelings of dismay or astonishment. The child cannot readily deal with the information so they remain aghast. Numbness might follow this feeling because it is a way the child has of preventing the extraordinary pain that the loss has induced.

Watching someone such as your beloved companion animal suffering on a daily basis might bring a sense of relief when that pet dies. The suffering experienced by pets is somewhat of an enigma. No one knows for sure how badly the pet is suffering but some of the outward signs certainly impress children emotionally. Whimpering, crying and not being able to stand, or possibly incontinence, are some of the obvious signs that a pet is ill. These signs sometimes come with age but a pet that has cancer or another terminal illness can also be seen suffering. Johnny came to my office telling me that when his dog Spot died he was so happy. The reason for his happiness was that the dog would no longer be suffering with his brain cancer. Johnny had seen Spot become disoriented and unable to walk. When the dog was euthanized Johnny was so relieved that he didn't have to watch his beloved pet endure the pain that the boy decided it was happiness he was feeling.

Anxiety is another feeling experienced by children in the wake of death. Anxiety often masks depression. It is that uneasy feeling associated with the dread that something bad is happening or going to happen. Children feel vulnerable to death after a death occurs and think that maybe someone else in the family will also die or maybe the child him or herself will die. This condition ushers forth anxiety which may be preparing the child for the impending feelings of depression and sadness.

What are some of the behaviors that can be observed in children following the loss of a pet?

Some of the most obvious behaviors seen in children after a loss of a pet include difficulty sleeping or nightmares, dreams of the lost pet, changes in eating habits, not wanting to disturb the personal effects of the deceased pet (such as water bowl, food dish or bed) as well as social withdrawal. Difficulty in sleeping is often seen after the loss of a significant other. It may be the result of depression or preoccupation with death (fear that death will come during the unconscious state of sleep).

Dreams of the lost pet are varied. These may be the result of the resolution of the loss if the child sees the pet happy and well and in a place that is pleasant. If the dreams become macabre, that is seeing the pet suffering or in a frightening condition, the child may be having a nightmare. Recently, a child of seven who had lost her dog a month earlier woke up in tears after having dreamt of the dog and wet her bed (an aberrant behavior for this child).

Eating too much out of anxiety or not eating as much out of sadness are both signs for concern in a child. Parents often use food to deal with emotions. Overeating or not eating are two such patterns which children model. Socialization by parents can lead to either one of these patterns when the child is suffering mourning and is grief ridden. Neither of these behaviors is acceptable if they last more than a week or so.

Some children feel comforted in seeing the personal effects of the pet left in place. It is the unconscious hope that the pet may return or it is just a comfort to see what belonged to the beloved pet still visible. Leaving food or water for the pet may be desired but not advisable. The pet's bed can also provide a source of comfort for the child.

Sometimes in children we see withdrawal from activities or events that they formerly enjoyed. Playing sports, having play dates or just solitary play may be interrupted for a period of time following the loss. Again, any prolonged period of this type of behavior should be dealt with professionally. It doesn't mean that a child is emotionally disturbed. It is most probably an adjustment reaction to a significant emotional upset.

Do children and adults experience the same stages of grief?

Sudden death of a pet and emotional isolation of the bereaved person are two indicators of stronger emotional reactions to the loss of a companion animal. Sharon, an eight-year-old third grader, kissed Rex good-bye as she always did before she left for school on a snowy day just before Christmas. While she was gone, her lovely young German shepherd ran out into the street and was killed by a passing automobile. Her father who was the stay-at-home parent buried Rex before Sharon returned from school. He thought he would spare her the pain of seeing her beloved dog. When seen in my office a week later on Christmas Eve, she was confused and feeling bewildered. Not only had she not been able to say good-bye to Rex but the day after his death her father went out and bought her a new puppy. She explained that she didn't know whether to laugh or cry. The new puppy was cute and cuddly but she still felt the presence of Rex around her. She felt that if she loved the new puppy she would be betraying her dog, Rex. Her isolation came in the fact that her parents did not know why she didn't feel happy. Cases of this kind can result in pathological mourning if the grief and mourning are left unresolved.

The stages of grief in the normal process of dying are described by the maverick of the field Elizabeth Kübler Ross (1969) as follows: denial and isolation; anger; bargaining; depression and acceptance. These stages are not only seen as stages for the person who is dying but also for those left bereft. Kübler Ross explains that not everyone goes through every stage and the stages are not always experienced in the order presented. For children grieving over the loss of their companion animal these stages are also present. As stated earlier, anger is often not seen toward the pet itself but may be toward the veterinarian or parent.

Companion animals do not leave their human companions with much ambivalence. Their love and loyalty is truly unmarred by defensive behaviors which oftentimes cause ambivalence in human relationships. Denial is very often seen when a pet is dying. Children refuse to believe that an animal so young or not appearing so sick is really going to die. When the death does in fact occur children are isolated in their grief as it is so difficult to find people in the circle of family and friends who really understand the closeness/attachment felt and grief experienced when that bond is broken.

When children hear that their pet is dying they often bargain with God to let their pet live. They promise any one of a variety of plans that they will complete so that God will spare the pet. Johnny (a 12-year-old) told me that when his cat, Frank, was dying he promised God to never curse again if Frank's life was spared. When Frank was eventually euthanized by the family veterinarian Johnny was enraged and accused the vet of killing Frank when he still was healthy. It took Johnny several weeks to finally accept that Frank was dead and deal with his grief. Johnny spoke of Frank in the present tense until he had accepted this event.

Chapter 4

Loss Occurs in Different Ways, Giving Rise to Varying Feelings

Reflection: **My Life with Bandit**
Scott Stekler

At two minutes to one on the day after Christmas, as the life drained out of his body, a part of me also died. Life would never be the same again. The dog that had brought incredible joy into my life was gone and I was grieving inconsolably. All that remained were numerous memories of our time together, time that was cut too short. I will hold on to these memories for the rest of my life. So today I write a story, a love story of sorts, a tribute to my dear and special friend. The following is a simple tale of a man and his dog.

My journey with Bandit began eight long years ago. He was a shelter dog who had been bounced from home to home. He was living with a family who brought him to me to cure his hacking cough. When I saw him that winter day I noticed that his glands were swollen and had suspected lymphoma, a form of cancer. His age was unknown but we estimated two to three years. He was young. The owner elected not to pursue his treatment and he was given to me. Bandit had found his final home.

He seemed like a sad sweet dog and I immediately began to treat his illness. I confirmed the diagnosis with a biopsy and started therapy shortly afterwards. He responded beautifully. His spirits and appetite picked up and he seemed content in his new home. In most cases, lymphoma is not a curable disease. The average dog only lives for roughly one year, so I was preparing myself for his demise. In his first few months with me I was growing quite attached to my shaggy friend. He was living in my office so we were always together. He loved playing with tennis balls and as often as possible we traveled to nearby parks to get some real exercise.

During our first summer together I realized how intelligent he was. My brother came by one day with his dog, Midnight. We were relaxing in the backyard and my brother began to boast how well trained his dog was. He instructed Midnight to "roll over." After several attempts he was giving up on Midnight's lack of enthusiasm and refusal to perform the trick. I then noticed, out of the corner of my eye, Bandit rolling over. I had never taught him any tricks. He just seemed to know.

Later that summer I introduced him to water. At first he was reluctant. It didn't take him long however, to become a natural swimmer. He was swimming as skillfully as the Labradors frolicking nearby. We frequented Harriman State Park and Lake Sebago was becoming his second home. Without encouragement he dove into the water looking for balls to retrieve. Bandit was paddling back to his master, his mouth engorged with tennis balls, sounding like the honking geese swimming with him. He seemed proud of his aquatic prowess and relinquished his toys on command. On one of these trips we hiked to a remote lake. It was incredibly hot outside and I foolishly chose to join Bandit in the water. On my way out I stepped on something soft near the edge of the water. A snake jumped out at me. After that incident, I let Bandit brave the waters alone.

The seasons changed and before long Bandit had been with me for over a year. There was no trace of his cancer. I was cautiously happy. Lymphoma is an unpredictable disease that could come back at any time. We were inseparable at this point and I couldn't imagine losing him. He visited my future in-laws at their apartment for a few hours. My future wife and I were going out and I thought that Bandit would enjoy their company. He quickly endeared himself to them by leaving his own personalized present on their living room rug. He had only three accidents in eight years. Nevertheless, we weren't allowed to leave him in their apartment again.

Bandit continued to remain healthy and after three years of therapy it became apparent that we had beat the lymphoma. In my fifteen years as a veterinarian, I have only "cured" two dogs. I certainly felt blessed. As my practice grew many of my days were busy and hectic. I looked forward to my relaxation time with Bandit. During the warmer months I spent many hours sitting outside basking in the sun while he preferred the shade. Although he was adept with tennis balls he never seemed to grasp the concept of frisbee. All of my efforts were fruitless. Luckily one of my clients was a tennis instructor. Bandit had a lifetime supply of tennis balls and didn't even realize it. So Bandit and I threw the frisbee away.

As a veterinarian I have had and continue to have a number of other pets. Bandit was never alone. It was not

unusual to see him licking and grooming one of our other
cats or dogs. It must have given him some sort of pleasure.
It also reinforced what a gentle dog he was. He could be
trusted with any tiny creature. They were always in good
hands with him. There was one thing, however, that you
could not trust Bandit with alone – food! He truly was a
bandit stealing any food within his reach. He was caught
red-handed on top of desks and bureaus, his head
crammed in garbage cans, all for the love of cat food. Cat
food was his culinary weakness and his hunger out-
weighed the repercussions of getting caught. It was futile
to reprimand him because he would only do it again after
a few days would lapse. His doe-like brown eyes made it
impossible to scold him. My wife would yell loudly, "No
Bandit, Bad Dog!" and then immediately turn to me and
say "Isn't it amazing how he can get up on the table like
that? God, is he smart!" It was clear that Bandit had full
reign of the household.

A month after we got married in the spring of 1996,
Bandit became very ill again. What started out slowly,
quickly developed into a life threatening condition. For
reasons I never discovered, Bandit had no platelets in his
blood. Without platelets, he was like a hemophiliac, prone
to bleeding. Inside his intestinal tract he bled uncontrolla-
bly. Day after day we treated him aggressively but nothing
seemed to slow the process down. What kept him alive
were frequent blood transfusions. He had 21 pints in all.
Unfortunately almost as quickly as he received the blood
his body was destroying it. He was transfused repeatedly
over a period of ten days. Towards the end of that period
my wife had to travel to southern New Jersey to obtain
more blood because the local animal hospitals could spare
no more. When all hope for recovery seemed bleak and
death seemed imminent, a miracle occurred. Slowly and

steadily Bandit began to produce platelets again. He gradually regained his strength and once again defied the odds. He had overcome two devastating illnesses and we didn't know if we were blessed or cursed. We were elated to have him back.

We resumed our park trips and he even accompanied me on errands around town. No trip seemed too short or long for him. He loved going for car rides and I enjoyed having him along. He was fine for a year before disease struck again. He started to violently sneeze and in the process his nose would drip blood. On a number of occasions we would return home to find blood splattered all over the kitchen or bedroom. After ruling out a platelet problem, we naturally thought the worst. Perhaps he had cancer that was eroding the lining of his nostrils. On two separate occasions we obtained tissue samples with the aid of an endoscope and anxiously awaited the biopsy results. To our delight, no cancer cells were seen. We removed a couple of teeth in the area and his newest condition resolved.

Soon after that episode we adopted an older Labrador retriever named Snickers. Bandit and Snickers became fast friends. On a daily basis we took them for a walk around the neighborhood. Snickers had come to us severely overweight and these walks were part of her weight loss program. She would walk quite slowly and occasionally Bandit would get frisky, grab her leash in his mouth, and pull her down the block. I would always get a big laugh whenever that happened. During this time we had developed a specific routine each morning. I would rise early to walk both dogs. I would let them back in the house while I retreated to my office to read the newspaper. When I returned to the bedroom I frequently found Bandit sleeping on my side of the bed. I guess he didn't want to waste a warm comfortable bed.

For the past two years, Bandit remained relatively disease free. He did develop a condition that made him very thirsty called Cushing's disease. However, the pills he took on a weekly basis controlled him nicely. I was beginning to feel that he was going to grow old with us. Unfortunately, that wasn't going to happen. Five days before Christmas, he stumbled during his evening walk. The next morning he had developed some minor neurological signs. I wasn't too worried at first. By midweek he had lost interest in food and his favorite treats. He began to pace and circle. On Christmas day he lost the ability to walk. I arrived at the grim conclusion that he had a brain tumor. I was heartbroken because I realized this was a battle I could not win. This happened so fast and I was not prepared to lose my best friend.

I always thought that the holidays were supposed to be filled with joy but I could feel no joy. I had to make an agonizing decision. His last night I slept by his side. It was a restless night for both of us. He was panting and I couldn't fall asleep. I tried to comfort him by holding his paw and telling him that he was going to be all right. I was uncertain if he could hear me because he may have been too delirious to realize I was there.

The next morning after a long discussion with my wife we arrived at the same conclusion. He wasn't going to recover and we thought that he was suffering. I couldn't allow him to suffer. Nothing in my life had been more difficult than putting him to rest. My hands shook and my body sobbed as I watched him take his last breath. He died peacefully in our arms and a sad calming and stillness had taken over the house. We could feel nothing but the warm tears running down our faces. I asked in disbelief what had we just done. My wife replied that we had made him better. I knew in my heart that he was running over that "Rainbow Bridge" but I wanted him here. I also know that he was at peace. In his eight years with me he brought me so much happiness. He enriched and changed my life and I loved him dearly. I only hope he knew that. When I laid him in his final resting place I said a prayer:

> I shall see Beauty
> But none to match your living grace.
> I shall hear music
> But none as sweet as the droning song
> With which you loved me
> I shall fill my days
> But I shall not, cannot forget
> Sleep soft, dear friend…

This chapter will discuss the differences in feelings experienced through the varying modes of loss. There are different feelings expected if a death was anticipated or sudden; whether the pet was euthanized; or whether the pet was lost through means other than death. Examples of the latter would be if the pet ran away from home or had to be given away because of inability to care for it or some human medical condition such as an allergy to the pet.

What are the different ways of losing a pet?

Death and loss (getting lost, stolen or running away) are two general ways of losing a pet. Death can come suddenly or as a result of an extended or short illness.

Companion pets in the US seem to die of many of the same illnesses as humans.

In the past, heart disease and bloating were common causes of death for many dogs. As we now have better remedies for these illnesses, dogs and cats are living longer. However, it is now estimated that it is cancer that kills half of old dogs and one-third of cats.

In a Danish study on the average lifespan and illnesses of different breeds of dog, the main cause of death was identified as "old age," killing over 20 percent of dogs (Proschowsky, Rugbjerg and Ersboll 2003). Other, less prevalent causes of death were accidents, heart disease and spinal disease.

Illness: Anticipated or expected

When dealing with death from illness, children seem to be able to grasp the concept as they transfer it from knowledge of human death from disease or old age. It is sad and painful but it has been seen by their friends or their parents in the loss of other human beings. Although some pets die suddenly of heart related illnesses or stroke, the majority die from cancers and other long-term illnesses.

When a pet dies from a sudden illness the impact is greater on those who love him or her. The first response is shock and disbelief. There is a thought that maybe there was a mistake. The companion animal may be young and the problem was not anticipated. A young woman in her late teens arrived at my office with her mother and younger sister. She had a four-year-old cat, Baby, who had recently died of a heart defect. The woman was inconsolable. She blamed herself for not seeing the symptoms but when using cognitive-behavioral therapy she saw that there was no known symptom that would have helped her to anticipate the outcome and that there was no remedy for the ailment. In a case like this it will take much time to overcome the grief, and the bereavement process will be difficult.

Numbness is another component of grief when there is a sudden loss. This occurs when the ego blocks feelings as a result of not being able to handle the underlying intense emotions. A high school student last saw her cat in the garden before the cat disappeared. A week later, the girl realized the cat was not coming home but was hard pressed to evoke the emotions that were just below the surface of her consciousness. These emotions sometimes appear when they are least expected and usually occur within months or possibly a year of the loss. A second grader in a local school had lost his dog and his mother brought him to see me because she feared his lack of emotional response. The family had a small ceremony to mark the death as well as looking over the pictures of the dog from his puppy years. Nothing seemed to evoke a response from seven-year-old Tommy. After the first visit to my office, Tommy went home and during the following weeks had a nightmare which awakened him. He dreamt that his dog, Nickey, was alive and they were running through the field where they had run years earlier. Tommy cried to his mother saying, "He was alive and healthy and now he is gone." The reality had broken through in a dream and now Tommy was able to deal with the feelings of grief and loss. It sometimes takes time for a child to deal with the feelings that have been suppressed.

There is no timetable or magical formula for this epiphany. It is an individual's ability to cope with the negative feelings that exist at the time that they arise. We can't coax the feelings out of the child but we must continue in a natural way speaking about the lost pet and allowing the feelings to arise when the child's psyche is ready.

In the process of death and the concomitant feelings that arise after someone you expect to die passes, there are many ways of dealing with the feelings. Sometimes shock, numbness and disbelief are part of the process as well. Other feelings that surface are sadness, anger, guilt, relief, helplessness and loneliness. The first symptoms of grief are usually the most intense and involve tightness in one's chest, sighing, uncontrollable crying, gasping for breath, headache, stomach aches and a myriad of physical sensations.

Euthanasia as a result of illness

When the veterinarian feels that no other means of helping the pet is possible and if palliative care is no longer working, the doctor might suggest euthanasia. Simply put – it is a means of ending life by chemical injection that is deemed humane and painless. Many pet owners accept this option as the best way of dealing with a dying pet. The decision for such a procedure should be made by the adults in the situation. The child in the family should never be given that responsibility. When such a decision is made, the adults need to communicate the information to the child in language that is comprehensible to the child. The child (as young as six years old) may be given the option of being present for the event. If the child decides not to be there, he or she should say "good-bye" to the pet beforehand. This is a very important concept. Saying good-bye helps the child deal with the finality of the occasion and relieves that guilt that occurs when a good-bye was not said. The way children terminate the relationship is important and parents should be the role model for them in these situations. If children choose not saying good-bye directly to the pet or if there is no time for such an experience, it would be helpful to draw a picture or paint an image of a good-bye scene. They might also write a good-bye letter to the pet as another option to the drawing.

Euthanasia for reasons other than illness

Only a fraction of the total number of pet deaths are a result of disease. Millions of companion animals are euthanized in the US each year because they are stray, abandoned, lost, ill-behaved, vicious, unable to be cared for by humans, or unwanted.

Death, for these causes, leaves people guilt ridden as well as bereft. Children especially are impotent in these decisions and may well wonder about parents' rationale for euthanizing the pet or for that matter giving it to a shelter. One very young child was anxiety ridden because his dog was euthanized for bad behavior. If Sam died because he was bad then what will happen to me if I'm bad or not doing what my parents want? It is a hard concept to challenge when a child transfers the rule to him or herself. It is also hard for a child to understand that the pet was euthanized. Questions that might be thought of but not asked may include: Does my pet feel pain or discomfort during this process? Is he or she afraid to die? Does my pet go to heaven (a special worry when the pet is euthanized for poor behavior)? Will I ever see him or her again? Do people get euthanized? Will I be euthanized if I'm bad or too hurt to be fixed?

These questions bring to mind the need for responsible pet ownership as well as the reality that euthanasia is a very common occurrence for our pets. Children respond to this type of loss either by withdrawing from pet ownership or by minimizing the importance of the pet to their existence. They also may become depressed or fearful that this fate might be their own as well. The concept of putting a pet to death, for reasons other than severe illness, is complex and defies reason for children. Too many pets and not enough people willing to care for them might easily be misconstrued as applying to children. That is, maybe Mommy and Daddy will send me away or worse "put me to sleep" because there are too many children in my family or in the world. It is concrete thinking but might be considered by children under the age of ten years since developmentally they are capable of concluding such a scenerio.

If the pet is given away because of a medical condition of a family member, the child might also be confused. "If my brother is allergic to Max and Max has to be given away, what if my brother becomes allergic to me?" Again this is concrete reasoning but such reasoning is quite common in the minds of children. Another sequence of events that could occur is that the pet must be given away because the child is allergic to it. If the child is attached to the pet, the feelings of guilt and loss would be intense. The child would then blame him or herself for the loss and be extremely saddened by the giving up of the pet. One six-year-old patient questions me by asking, "Why do I have to be allergic? I love cats and want to touch my Fluffy and she really makes me feel good and now I won't even be able to see her anymore." Sadness, guilt and anger are the emotions experienced in this situation. Parents must try to allay the guilt and if the pet is given to another family must try to help the child visualize where the pet will be and that he or she will have a good life. Again, writing a letter to the pet or writing to the new owner might be helpful to the child.

What happens when a pet runs away?
This process really leaves children uncertain about the pet's fate or whether or not the pet will return. Responsible adults should do all that they can to try and retrieve the lost pet. Calling the local police, visiting the pound, and putting up signs as well as sending fliers through the neighborhood are effective ways of retrieving a lost pet. Being honest with children at a time like this is important. You may fantasize that the pet has a new home and present a "rosy" picture to the children but asking them what they think and validating their response is quite important. You might ask the child to draw a picture of "Fido" as pictured in the place that he now is. Let children talk about the fantasy even if it is negative. Don't try and deny the children's thoughts about the whereabouts of their pet. The feelings involved in this type of loss for children are very confusing and often leave them with unresolved feelings about the pet. The child does not know when or if to grieve since the pet might return.

Chapter 5

Pet Replacement?

Reflection: **Can you Buy Love?**
JoAnn Jarolmen

"Whoever said you can't buy love or happiness must not
have known the love of a puppy." This I quote from a
life-altering email that I received from my veterinarian
containing pictures of recently retrieved shar-pei puppies
from China. Shar-pei are one of the most sought-after
breeds. They are irresistible with their sensual looks and
inviting wrinkles but they are also at risk for amazingly
complex and serious physical problems which are a nightmare for them and their owners.

At one time, I had four shar-pei: a mother and three
of her pups. Last year, I lost the last of the pups, a
14-year-old male, Lucci, who was born in my home.
Three of the four died of lymphoma. I hadn't been to the
vet's office since Lucci died, but on that fateful August day
I arrived with two of my cats for their yearly visit. Dr.
Linda Tintle of Wurtsboro, New York told me she wanted
me to meet someone before we got started treating the
cats. Myrtle the Turtle walked into the room and a feeling
of exuberance overcame me. I hadn't felt that way in many
a moon. She was a lovely wrinkled shar-pei with an

affable disposition who Dr. Tintle had acquired after her
recent trip to China. The doctor, who has owned and
taken special care of shar-pei for years, then told me she
was expecting three young pups to arrive from China in a
week. This brings me to my initial statement: I saw the
pictures of the puppies and immediately fell in love.

Dr. Tintle asked me if I wanted to participate in joint
ownership of one of these pups. It seemed that she and
some very interested ethical breeders want to improve the
breed in this country and sought lines in China that may
not have the same flawed genes that are common here.
She hoped that the American-type shar-pei could be
helped by studying these original traditional dogs from
mainland China that appeared free from the disorders that
plagued their western cousins. I pondered the question
and my answer was an ambivalent, "no."

The day after my decision, a frantic call from my
daughter about an accident that occurred with her new
French Bulldog pup, Marcel, brought me on a journey to
Dr. Tintle's office that would change my life. After the
crisis with Marcel was quickly dispatched with superb
expertise by Dr. Tintle, I asked her if she had received my
email. She very nonchalantly said she had. I then asked if
the puppies were there and she said they were. Did I want
to see one? I couldn't resist. An adorable puppy in the
arms of Dr. Tintle arrived in the room. She was, without a
doubt, the quintessential shar-pei. She was about eight
inches long, weighing about four pounds, with a soft,
round belly and adorned with a very lovely horsecoat. Dr.
Tintle placed her in my arms. As she looked up at me I
could feel my heart melt. Her innocence and warmth
enveloped me. Her languishing brown eyes beckoned me
to bring her home. She kissed me and it was all over. I
was hers. I told the doctor I would still have to think

about it since I'm not an impulsive or "love at first sight" kind of person. The next morning I was compelled with a strange polarization to my computer where without hesitation I emailed my affirmative answer and waited to see if I was still acceptable. Alas, I was. I named my new pup Francesca (a name chosen by her European uncle and godfather, Christian). Needless to say, after a day or two of preparation Francesca came home with me and now my bundle of shar-pei joy is growing in size and love with me. She has renewed my life and lifted my spirits to new heights. Well, maybe you can buy love.

Pet replacement

This section addresses the timely and appropriate "replacement" of a pet. The when, where, and who of a new pet to be brought into the home will be discussed. It has been seen that those individuals who replace a pet during the first year, especially in the first one- to four-month interval after the loss of the pet, have more grief to deal with than those who do not. I have explored the kind of pet chosen and who would be involved in the selection process. My observations make sense since when grief is unresolved, it is highly unlikely for a person to invest emotionally in a parallel relationship.

According to *Webster's Unabridged Dictionary* (1997), replacement is defined as: "A person or thing that takes the place of another, especially of one that has worn out, broken down, etc." Is this what you want when a beloved member of your family dies or is gone forever? When we assess replacement in terms of the real meaning of the word, most of us don't feel comfortable considering a replacement for our lost pet or for that matter any other family member or friend.

Freud talks about detaching hopes and memories from the lost object in order to be able to reinvest that psychic energy into another relationship. I don't believe that one can erase memories of a beloved being that has been lost. Retaining memories of the lost love object is important for the healthy resumption of life. The task at hand is relocating the energy (from the lost relationship) into a new relationship. This task can only be achieved by reformulating life with that person or being placed in perspective. That is, not thinking of them in the present and not relying on their response to our lives. The memories of the deceased will always remain but the emotional life of the survivor must resume and love, hope and joy must re-enter the conscious emotions for life to progress. Sadness over the loss may last for the rest of one's life but allowing oneself to love again is essential for the healthy resolution of mourning and resumption of life's activities. The process of mourning must be experienced and resolved in order to reinvest one's psychic energy into another relationship.

One holiday evening, I received a frantic call from a young lady who had lost her dog two days earlier. She had left her home in the morning to go to school. She said good-bye to her young, mixed-breed dog, Bill. He was well and happy as she left for school that day. When she returned from school, she was told by her father that Bill had been killed by a truck during the day and he had taken him to the veterinarian for disposal. The young adolescent was devastated. She couldn't believe that her healthy, loving pet had been killed and was already disposed of. She would never see him again or be able to say good-bye. She mourned all night for him. The next day her father surprised her with a new puppy. That puppy was an golden retriever. When she arrived at my office, she told me she didn't know whether to laugh or cry. She still heard the footsteps of her beloved lost dog and thought she heard him bark that night but was occupied by the new puppy that needed attention and love. She was truly torn and tormented by the situation. She had not had the time to mourn for the lost pet nor had she been able to say good-bye to him. She needed to resolve her feelings over her loss before she could reinvest her emotions in the new puppy. I suggested that she write a letter to Bill to explain how she felt. I also suggested a memory box so that she might always have his effects separate and with her.

The role the survivor experienced with the lost love object can be resumed and should be resumed over time. The emptiness felt by the survivor can only be filled by resuming that role in some fashion. If one tries to re-assume that role with a "replacement" object, comparisons will always be made to the predecessor. It is often said that after a pet dies, the next pet should be a different breed or another type of pet so that comparisons are less likely to be made. The new pet usually loses when competition or comparison is set up between the old and new pet. We tend to remember only the good parts of a lost or deceased love object. Therefore the new pet pales in contrast to the old. It is important not to compare.

When we take time to feel the feelings we have for the lost love object, we realize that part of our emotional life will always be invested in that love relationship and we cannot forget the deceased being. Our memories will evoke both love and sadness when we recall the specific days and times that are outstanding in our life with the love object. Keep in mind that this is a normal reaction and should be validated. Children as well as adults respond to the loss of a love object in the same way. Oftentimes, they do not have the verbal skills to express these feelings so drawing or writing a letter sometimes can help them get to those feelings. Even acting it out can help. Dorothy, a ten-year-old girl, came to my office after the loss of her dog. After a month or so, she and her friends were writing a story. Her part in this story encompassed the life of a girl with her dog. She wrote about her nightly talks with him, her walks with him and playing ball with him in the backyard. These memories even when written in a fictional setting were cathartic.

When is the appropriate time to get a new pet?

This is a difficult question to answer as there is no set recipe for the best time to get a new pet. It depends on the emotional investment in the lost pet as well as other variables that might come into play with the person(s) who have experienced the loss. For instance, in my experience a child who had lost another significant other to death, divorce or because of relocation would have a harder time with the initial loss of the pet because the loss would be confounded. A little girl was very saddened by the loss of both her dog and her grandfather within the same month. In this case it would take longer for her to reinvest her feelings in a new relationship since she first needs to mourn the losses. As discussed in Chapter 4, it also depends on whether or not the death was anticipated or expected. The circumstances of death all contribute to the resolution of the grief process.

The average time it takes to complete the mourning process is about one year. At times, it takes longer and sometimes it is shorter. It really depends on the individual. A family I saw had lost their dog after a terrible accident. The dog's death was quite horrible with gore and blood all around the whimpering, suffering pet. One of the three children blamed himself for the loss because he had opened the door when the dog ran out and was hit by the car. Now, as a young adult, he has vowed never to have another pet. He claims he doesn't like pets but it is obvious that the guilt remains from that bitter loss. The family unit was not ready to get another pet until seven years after that death. The young man was not involved with that new pet. Eventually, they got a dog that was very different and had a wonderful relationship with her. There was the readiness factor that permitted them from reinvesting their emotions in this new dog.

Another variable which might affect the addition of a new pet is the emotional connection with the lost pet. The closer the emotional attachment the more difficult and prolonged the mourning and bereavement would be. Sometimes, the shock is so great that the grief work cannot begin until the emotional being of the person is ready to accept the pain. This phenomenon is particularly common in children.

Whether or not the death was sudden or anticipated also influences the length of mourning. In sudden deaths the emotional working through of feelings would be more difficult. When a death is anticipated, the person can say their good-byes, give all the love and affection that they need to express, imagine what life would be like without the pet and sometimes even feel at peace when the event occurs. A pet that will be euthanized can be given his or her favorite food or get involved in a favorite activity. A young girl, Molly, had a sick cat named Spike. Spike was an old cat who was tough but the family knew that he was going downhill. Molly knew that his favorite food was Mom's meatloaf. She feed him that meatloaf by hand until the day came when he was not able to eat any longer and the veterinarian recommended that he be euthanized. When Molly drew a picture of Spike in my office, it was fondly recalling those days before he died when she fed him that meatloaf. Another child, Tom, who was 13 years old, had a labrador retriever whose behavior had become problematic and because of all the erratic behavior the parents made the decision to have him euthanized. Before going to the veterinarian's office for the final time, Tom played a game of catch with his dog (which they had done together since the dog was a pup). The child remembered that scene and was able to mourn the loss with the satisfaction that he had given his dog one last happy event. These anticipated deaths are very hard to deal with before the death but make the process of bereavement and mourning less difficult.

What kind of pet should we get after the mourning process?

Today I spoke to a little girl named Julia. She lost her cat two weeks ago in the country where her family has a home. The cat ran out of the house and for two days the family scoured the countryside but did not find the cat.

The child's mother felt helpless, hopeless and guilty for the loss. When I asked Julia if she had found her cat she dejectedly said, "No" but added that she got another one. Her affect was flat as she told me and seemed to have no reaction to the new cat. Even after I asked how big the cat was and wished her well with her new pet, she had no emotional reaction. Julia, in common with many other children her age, may not have been ready to talk about her feelings of loss but then how could she get in touch with her feelings of joy over the new pet? I'm not sure how her feelings will play out or when she will deal with them but the joy of a new pet was certainly not sensed in my conversation with her.

It does not matter what kind of pet you choose when you are ready to extend your love and energy to another companion animal. The rule of thumb is not to get exactly the same type of pet or the same color. These cautions are in place so that you will not have the same expectations for the new pet. When we expect to "replace" a pet and hope that we will no longer remember the lost pet, we are fooling ourselves. Or when we think giving the pet the same name or having a pet that looks exactly like the lost one will fulfill our wish for the return of the lost pet, we are trying to create fiction. Our children should also be cautioned not to create fiction and realize that the new member of our family is not the deceased member nor is it a substitute for the lost pet.

A new pet should not be bought on an impulse. It should be well thought out and planned. New pets should never be a surprise unless you are sure that the person(s) involved is ready for this new love and responsibility. Children's feelings must be considered in the course of getting a new pet. As demonstrated in the case of the little girl who had a passive reaction to the new cat, I think we should be sure that the children involved have successfully resolved the mourning process before a new pet is brought into the home. As I mentioned before, children are not on the same timetable as adults in the grieving process. It often takes them longer to begin the grief period. Always be sure to take all members of the family into consideration before bringing a new member to the family unit.

Chapter 6

The Journey Back

Reflection just for fun: **Babysitting Sonny**
Michael Ardizzone

He was a few weeks old and weighed less than a pound. I weighed 185. Still, I was no match for Sonny, a kitten named after James Caan's character in "The Godfather." It was no contest. He knocked me out.

On the weekend in question, his keeper, JoAnn, had to be out of town and I was "on call" for kitten-sitting duty. When she asked me to take Sonny for the weekend, I jumped at the chance. "An inconvenience? Of course not. I've taken care of dozens of kittens." After all, who wouldn't want to take care of a beautiful ball of fur?

JoAnn has rescued many stray cats and establishes a special bond with each one. When I picked up Sonny for the weekend, she left me with an endless list of instructions, typical of an overprotective parent: "Make sure his formula is heated...but don't overheat it. If he gets the runs, mash two grains of rice in this food. See that he doesn't catch cold, but try not to use the space heater..." And on and on. I shrugged it off. How difficult could this be? But as her list got longer and longer, I got more worried. I was used to caring for kittens who were at least six weeks old and basically able to care for themselves. Maybe this wasn't going to be so easy after all.

Three-week-old kittens, like human babies, have to be fed every four hours with formula from a bottle...even in the middle of the night. Even their waste has to be induced. That weekend I learned two things: I'm lucky I escaped with my sanity, and I'll never make a good father. But on that particular weekend, fatherhood was on the agenda, 24 hours a day.

A big part of the nightmare had to do with feeding Sonny. I gave him carefully heated kitten formula in a makeshift little baby bottle. The awkward transfer from heated saucepan to tiny bottle caused most of the formula to overflow and decorate my shirt. The transfer to Sonny's mouth was equally clumsy, causing most of his chin and throat to be coated with milky formula that should have found its way to his stomach. What's worse, JoAnn instructed me not to bathe him, fearing he'd catch cold. After just a few feedings, his little body was almost completely glazed over with dried formula.

I also spoon-fed him with a mixture of moist kitten food and baby food, with two grains of rice. Even though I left the rest of the food for him to nibble at, he insisted on being fed by hand. He still wasn't comfortable with finding his own food and eating it without help. Setting the alarm every four hours was also a harrowing experience. During that entire weekend, I never knew what hour of the day or night it was. All I knew was that when the alarm went off and Sonny was crying, it had to be time to heat up the formula.

When he was quiet, Sonny was irresistible. His navy blue eyes and waif-like appearance made him seem innocent and vulnerable. He was a stray, an orphan. That weekend, I was all he had in the world. He was so small I could hold him easily in one hand. His soft, gray-striped fur was still silky, like a newborn. He was a minor miracle...and a little terror. When he was hungry or playful, he was as unbearable as he was cute, like an angel gone berserk. He refused discipline and was proud of it. His nails and teeth were like razors in search of human flesh. Like Sonny Corleone, he had a short temper and demanded immediate gratification – even when he wasn't sure what he wanted. No matter how upset I got at him, every time he cried, my paternal instincts kicked in and I panicked. "What does he want now?" "Is he chilly?" "Did I do something wrong?" After all, I was his lifeline.

My weekend with Sonny left me with an enormous amount of respect for mother cats. Queens have to deal with five or six of these restless little dynamos, each one biting, crying, feeding, messing – for at least six weeks. I don't know how they cope. I could barely deal with one of them for a single weekend. And I don't even want to think about the commitment needed for human babies.

Much to my surprise, I did survive. And so did Sonny. He didn't starve, or catch pneumonia, or suffer any of the terrible things I imagined would happen. On the other hand, I didn't get much sleep until I took Sonny back to JoAnn's that Sunday night. I was a reluctant and fumbling godfather, but I hope that in some small way, I was able to show him enough affection and care to help him get going in life.

I have since paid Sonny several visits. He's doing quite well at JoAnn's house. Taking care of a kitten was the best introduction to parenting I could hope for. And the worst weekend I could imagine. It's difficult, messy and ruins many a good night's sleep. Still, I strongly recommend it. There's nothing like holding a life in the palm of your hand.

This chapter includes personal vignettes of my practice as well as comments and conclusions. One common element that is seen in practice when dealing with the loss of a companion animal is that of isolation. Young and old and in-between-aged people always have a sense of isolation when losing their pet. It is hard to find a sympathetic ear and heart which are essential in getting through the grief process. Those who grieve alone are more susceptible to depression, prolonged grief, pathological mourning, and sadness.

Why are people isolated in their grief after the loss of a pet?

A major problem about death, grief and mourning is the fact that the subject is taboo in our society. Death is often a sterile process usually in an antiseptic room with white curtains drawn. No one model of grief or death is ever talked about. Our society spells out denial as the most acceptable method of facing death. We dole out time periods from days to months as to how long a person is supposed to grieve over lost friends and relatives. Few people even discuss the loss of a companion animal with any validity as to the grief process experienced. Instead people who grieve openly for the lost pet are often made to feel eccentric, inappropriate, weak, nullified, absurd and/or crazy. Since society "disenfranchises" this type of grief, only those who have experienced it can give empathy and solace. Those who do are vulnerable to the same kind of response as those who have lost their pet. That is, isolation, ridicule and ostracism are often experienced by both those who are mourning and those who give them support and empathy.

Each time I see someone for the problems of grief after the loss of a companion animal the similar complaints are heard. For example:

1. Get over it, it was only an animal.

2. Why don't you just go out and replace it and that will make you feel better?

3. I think you should only feel like that if a human dies.

4. People are going to think you are weird if you cry over a pet.

5. Ha ha! Is that what you're crying about?

6. No, you may not take a bereavement day off because your pet died. Your pay will be docked if you don't come to work.

As soon as the grief is validated, people are freed to experience the difficult feelings they are having and thereafter work through the grief process. I often am asked if it is all right to cry over the loss of a pet. Of course it is. Once catharsis begins, the grief ensues and the process of re-engaging in life begins.

What is the reaction of children who are grieving for a lost pet?
Younger children are not restrained by society's taboos until adults impose them on the child. I remember treating an 11-year-old girl, Jane, whose two-year-old cat and best friend in the whole world had died. This cat, Tiger, had contracted some quick-moving virus and was dead within

a few hours. Jane was alone at home when the disaster occurred. She was devastated. When her father came home from work, he yelled at her very angrily and told her she was not permitted to cry over the cat. She didn't know what to do with her sad and languishing feelings so it resulted in a reactive depression which had to be treated in therapy. Had this young girl and many others like her been permitted to grieve and given validation and empathy for their loss, depression may well have been averted. Normal grief is an expected process and a natural one that is experienced after a significant loss. The significance of the loss is determined by the emotional reaction of the grieving individual.

Not all children react to a loss of a pet the same way. One day at school, a mother called me about her three teenagers who were coming in to see me because their dog had died suddenly the night before. The oldest of the three was very mature and concerned about her younger siblings. The boy who was the middle child was the most consumed with grief at the time. I remember writing notes to their teachers to explain the loss and how the children were feeling on that day. The children came back at the end of the day and said that they were given support, empathy and concern from all of the teachers and students alike. They were feeling better and then returned home to their parents who were also feeling sad and could share their feelings with their children. It was a very good resolution to a very sad situation.

Another child came to school one day devastated because her pet bird had frozen to death the night before. Denise was a very sensitive child from a single-parent home. Her mother was a secretary for a local company but was having trouble paying her bills since money was tight and her ex-husband was a "dead beat dad." The bird froze because the heat and electricity had been turned off due to failure of bill payment. Denise was enraged with her mother and blamed her for the bird's death but when the tragedy of their lives was pointed out they both understood that they as well as the bird were victims and they shared their grief with each other.

I became known as the grief counselor and teachers as well as students would seek my help when a pet loss occurred. Most children did not need counseling if the death and subsequent grief were treated appropriately by the adults surrounding them. Taking the time to be empathic, caring and validating are very important factors no matter what the loss is. A problem arises when adults make value judgments on the grief for an animal. One little eight-year-old girl who needed to be nurtured, and as a result did a great deal of it for others, was crying after the death of her pregnant fish. Maggie had become attached to the fish that her mother bought for her because the little girl wanted a baby sister or brother. While the child was at church one Sunday, the pregnant fish jumped out of the bowl and died. The child not only mourned for the lost pet but for the unborn baby fish which she was so looking forward to nurturing. These were the substitute brothers or sisters she longed for. The family made fun of her and the child became depressed. "It was only a fish," was the retort. Those around her did not realize the true significance of this fish in that child's life. Again, who are we to judge how someone should feel? Our feelings are not logical and don't come from a reasonable source. They are our unique feelings and remain to be dealt with, not made fun of, controlled or destroyed.

Chapter 7

Conclusions

"Give sorrow words. The grief that does not speak
Whispers the o'erfraught heart and bids it break."

(*Macbeth*, William Shakespeare)

Reflection: **Cats, Friendships, and the Bonds that Break**
JoAnn Jarolmen and Michael Ardizzone

Cats can be a way of bringing people together. Our feline
friends not only create bonds between themselves and
people, they can forge bonds between humans. For
instance, we would have never met our friend Janet if it
weren't for our mutual love of cats. Janet got John's phone
number through the grapevine as someone who could
help her rescue the "mama" cat and kittens that lived
outside Janet's condo. When we first arrived at Indian
Hollow Condominiums, we found Janet outside in the
cold trying to lure two young cats into a makeshift shelter
she had devised. We soon discovered that Janet was a
warm, good-natured person who felt almost hopeless
about the circumstances of the strays in her care. She
worried about them endlessly, saying "Do you think they

will freeze outside?" She fixed boxes with blankets and towels to serve as temporary shelters until the day we successfully rescued all the cats.

Unfortunately, the kittens were no longer kittens. Scooter, Winston, Little Bit and Daisy, the first of several litters we rescued there, had almost reached maturity. It would take all of our humane traps, many nights, and lots of tuna to catch them.

We soon found that Janet had a hidden talent for scouting out and finding good homes – often a much tougher task than actually catching the cats. In fact, homes were waiting for many of them when they finally were caught. Janet took pictures of the kittens to many local veterinary offices and became a successful adoption counselor. If the kitten was unattractive, Janet would use the selling point, "What he or she doesn't have in looks, he or she makes up in personality." Her work was so impressive. She thoroughly enjoyed her new job. Janet was persistent and focused on her mission. She was also becoming a true friend.

Single and childless, Janet had three cats who were her kids. After her early retirement, Janet devoted all her time, love and money to her beautiful Maine coon cats. She took on a fourth who was one of the strays and quite a handful. She pampered and coddled them all, saying, "I take better care of my cats than myself." But even her loving care couldn't save one of her beloved cats who died in August, 1995. Her words and her loss were a foreshadowing. Unbeknownst to any of us, Janet was also near her end. She was diagnosed with inoperable cancer in August of 1996 and died three months later.

The personal tragedy of her death was compounded by the uncertain futures of her cats. Our friend, who loved her cats so much and who had found homes for many strays, certainly would have wanted her cats to be together in a carefully chosen, loving home. But when her fatal illness struck, she did not have the strength, health or mental wherewithal to find homes for her own cats. As we remember and mourn our friend, we've learned some valuable lessons: Love, your friends, human and animal. Do your best to give comfort to those in need – the way your pets do when you need solace. Make provisions for them in the event of your passing. Do your homework so you won't be leaving your beloved pets abandoned, as there are many resources for just this inevitability.

In this concluding chapter I summarize the components necessary for the successful completion of bereavement in children and help adults to see the importance of helping children deal with these issues. I also list the most important issues to explore with children after the loss of a companion animal.

As discussion and acceptance in this area of loss especially with children is new, education and honest exploration of feelings is essential for children to successfully navigate through the process. When I first began my work in grief and bereavement 20 years ago, these issues were taboo. We were not allowed to investigate children's feelings when it came to death, grieving or bereavement. Some felt that children were immune to the feelings of grief and others felt that children did not understand death so they could not really grasp the impact of the loss; still others felt that we would damage children emotionally by discussing the subject of death and grief. These statements refer only to death and loss in general. The area of pet loss and bereavement was even more obscure and looked upon as strange in terms of psychotherapy. We naively looked at the lost object as not human and therefore not valued as much as a human. We failed to recognize the issues of attachment and loss. The fact of the matter is, when you lose an attachment figure, the depth of the attachment to the lost object predicts the depth and length of the grief and mourning that ensue. Only through the development of empirical information have we arrived at the validation of this conception.

The history of the professional examination of grief and bereavement goes back to the 1940s. It seems that after significant tragedies professionals begin to explore the components of a phenomenon. In the 1940s, we saw a fire that killed hundreds of people and we then began to look at the emotional composition of the aftermath of that event. During World War II, children in England were left in orphanages either so their parents could help in the war effort or because the children were orphaned by the war. At that time attachment was examined and an understanding of the grief process of children began. With the changes in our family and societal structure, there were unique relationships that evolved especially after the social revolution of the 1960s. The idea of people responding and grieving for the loss of friendships other than family and friends introduced the concept of "disenfranchised grief". This grief was about losses that people were not expected to grieve such as former mates, gay partners, and companion animals. In the 1980s we began to look at the grief after the loss of a pet. It was mostly recognized by veterinarians and people in the pet world. Adults were the subject of most investigations on this issue. After the World Trade Center tragedy and its aftermath, we now realize that children as well as adults grieve for lost relationships and we realize that their experience is unique.

In light of the above summarized history, the experience of my life's practice is not surprising. The grief experienced by children has been found to be significantly deeper than that of the adults. I have observed the deepest grief in those people who lost their pets between one and four months prior to participation in the treatment process. There was also a difference in the intensity and length of grief shown based on whether or not the death was anticipated. Those who had not anticipated the loss had more deeply felt grief symptoms than those who had. The people who brought a new pet into the home immediately had more guilt and grief than those who waited until a time when the grief had subsided.

The steps in the process of grief are fairly individualized. Knowing that certain feelings are to be expected can help you deal with yourself and your child when these events occur. Feelings of sadness, anger, guilt, anxiety, loneliness, fatigue, helplessness, shock, relief and numbness are all normal and should be allowed to be expressed. If a caretaker feels that these expressions of feeling are exaggerated or prolonged then professional help or guidance should be sought. It is hard to see our children suffering but cutting the process short or trying to inhibit the child's response could progress into more serious emotional difficulty. Allow your child to be him or herself and be there to support his or her needs. This is the substance of true compassion.

The ten most important facts to keep in mind when dealing with children's loss:

1. Be honest. No mollification or deception especially about going to "sleep."

2. Permit your child to ask questions. Don't be afraid of what they ask. You can always admit that you don't know the answer but are willing to find out.

3. Allow your child to say good-bye. We always feel that we need to protect our kids from reality but the basic truth is that they need to experience the finality of the loss and have closure, just like you.

4. Permit your child the opportunity to express his or her feelings. You can let them cry without minimizing the loss.

5. Show your child that you, too, feel very sad. Don't be afraid to cry in front of your child.

6. If at first the child seems withdrawn, remember, it's not about the absence of feelings. It may just be that he or she cannot allow the feelings to surface.

7. Remember, there is no time limit to the beginning or the end of grief.

8. Be vigilant. The child sometimes tries to protect you by not letting you see them grieve.

9. If your pet is terminally ill, allow your child to talk about what it will be like not having "Fido" or "Fluffy" around.

10. When the death is sudden or accidental, remember this experience may be more intense for the child; so don't be surprised by the reaction.

Bibliography

Ardizzone, M. "A sudden death and longstanding grief." Unpublished.

Ardizzone, M. (1992) "Babysitting Sonny." *Cats Magazine 49*, 3, 32.

Averill, J. (1968) "Grief: Its nature and significance." *Psychological Bulletin 70*, 6, 721–748.

Beck, A. and Katcher, A. (1984) *Between Pets and People.* New York: Perigee Books.

Bowlby, J. (1963) "Pathological mourning and childhood mourning." *Journal of the American Psychoanalytic Association 11*, 500–541.

Bowlby, J. (1973) *Attachment and Loss, Volume II: Separation.* New York: Basic Books.

Bowlby, J. (1977) "The making and breaking of affectional bonds." *British Journal of Psychiatry 130*, 201–210.

Bowlby, J. (1980) *Attachment and Loss, Volume III: Loss.* New York: Basic Books.

Bowlby, J. (1988) *A Secure Base.* New York: Basic Books.

Brasted, E. and Callahan, E. (1984) "A behavioral analysis of the grief process." *Behavior Therapy 15*, 529–543.

Chill, A. "For the love of Looie." Unpublished.

Dahm, P.C. (1998) *The Rainbow Bridge.* Oceanside, OR: Running Tide Press.

Doka, K. (1989) *Disenfranchised Grief.* New York: Lexington Books.

Holcomb, R., Williams, R. and Richards, P. (1985) "The elements of attachment: Relationship maintenance and intimacy." *Journal of the Delta Society 2*, 1, 28–34.

Jarolmen, J. "Can you buy love?" Unpublished.

Jarolmen, J. and Ardizzone, M. (1997) "Cats, friendships, and the bonds that break." *Interactions 15*, 3, 8.

Kübler Ross, E. (1969) *On Death and Dying.* New York: Macmillan.

Lindemann, E. (1994) "Symptomatology and management of acute grief." *American Journal of Psychiatry 151*, 6, 155–160.

Melson, G. (1988) "Availability and involvement with pets by children: Determinants and correlates." *Anthrozoos 2*, 1, 45–52.

Melson, G. (1990) "Studying children's attachment to their pets: A conceptual and methodological review." *Anthrozoos 4*, 2, 91–99.

Proschowsky, H.F., Rugbjerg, H. and Ersboll, A.K. (2003) "Mortality of purebred and mixed-breed dogs in Denmark." *Preventive Veterinary Medicine 58*, 1, 630–674.

Raphael, B. (1983) *The Anatomy of Bereavement.* New York: Basic Books.

Rusk, A. (2005) "Cancer: Cases likely will rise in aging animals." *DVM Newsmagazine*, 1 Mar. www.dvmnewsmagazine.com/dvm

Stekler, S. "My life with Bandit." Unpublished.

Weisman, A.S. (1991) "Bereavement and companion animals." *Omega 22*, 4, 241–248.

Worden, J.W. (1991) *Grief Counseling and Grief Therapy.* New York: Springer Publishing Company.

Useful resources

Helpful websites

www.deltasociety.org/PetLossArticles.htm
This helpful website includes a full list of services dealing with the human–animal bond.

www.pet-loss.net/links.html
This site has a full resource of state by state support groups, resources and counselors.

www.nepanetwork.com/pets.htm
Here you will find a list of pet loss support resources.

www.vetmed.ucdavis.edu/ccab/petloss.html
This site is the University of California at Davis. It has a comprehensive list of support for people going through pet loss. It even has a hotline.

http://exoticpets.about.com
This site deals with the loss of exotic pets.

www.cvm.uiuc.edu/CARE/
University of Illinois College of Veterinary Medicine. C.A.R.E. Pet Loss Helpline.

www.tufts.edu/vet/petloss
Tufts University pet loss support hotline.

http://web.vet.cornell.edu/public/petloss/
Cornell University pet loss support hotline.

www.aplb.org
The Association for Pet Loss and Bereavement non-profit pet loss group.

http://cvm.msu.edu/petloss/index.htm
Michigan State University pet loss support resources.

www.vetmed.iastate.edu/animals/petloss/
Iowa State University pet loss hotline.

www.vetmed.wsu.edu/PLHL/home/index.asp
Washington State University pet loss support on-line.

www.afn.org/~afn26752/phone.html
Helpful phone numbers for pet lovers including pet loss support.

www.catsunited.com/html/pet_loss.html
Cats United Services is a resource for those who have suffered the loss of a cat.

www.fourpawsinheaven.com/links/links.html
An on-line pet memorials link page.

www.lightning-strike.com/pet-loss-books.htm
A resource of pet loss books.

www.geocities.com/Heartland/Bluffs/2625/
A pet loss support group of Ottawa, Canada.

www.petplace.com/dogs/coping-with-pet-loss/page1.aspx
Pet Place is an on-line resource for sharing in pet loss.

http://handicappedpets.com/memorial/cemetary.htm
A website listing cemeteries and crematoriums for pets.

www.aahanet.org/common/products/displayproductlist_v2.cfm?&C
GRFNBR=46&CRPCGNBR=42&TextMode=0&CI=1
This is the American Animal Hospital Association's website for pet loss.

www.cdc.gov/healthypets/resources/websites.htm
The CDC website for pet care.

http://vetmedicine.about.com/od/lossandgrief/
A veterinary website for resources dealing with pet loss.

Suggested reading

Please note that a few of the titles listed may not be cur-
rently available, however it may be possible to special order
through a major bookshop or look for them at a local
library. Most titles have been found on-line/in store.

Pet loss

Adamec, C. (2000) *When Your Pet Dies*. New York, NY: Berkley Pub Group.

Anderson, M. (1996) *Coping with Sorrow on the Loss of Your Pet*. Crawford, CO: Alpine Publications, Inc.

Bronson, H. (2000) *Dog Gone: Coping with the Loss of a Pet*. Sandwich, MA: Bestsell Publications.

Carmack, B.J. (2002) *Grieving the Death of a Pet*. Minneapolis, MN: Augsburg Fortress Publishers.

Kay, W.J., Kutscher, A.H., Fudin, C.E., Nieburg, H, Grey, R.E. and Cohen, S.P. (eds) (1988) *Euthanasia of the Companion Animal: Its Impact on Pet Owners, Veterinarians, and Society*. Philadelphia, PA: Charles Press Publishers.

Kay, W.J., Kutscher, A.H., Fudin, C.E., Nieburg, H.A., Kutscher, L. and Grey, R.M. (eds) (1988) *Pet Loss and Human Bereavement*. Iowa, IA: Iowa State University Press.

Kosins, M.S. (1996) *Maya's First Rose: Diary of a Very Special Love*. New York, NY: Berkley Pub Group.

Lagoni, L.S., Butler, C. and Hetts, S. (1994) *The Human-Animal Bond and Grief*. Philadelphia, PA: W.B. Saunders Publishing.

Lee, L. and Lee, M. (2003) *Absent Friend: Coping with the Loss of a Treasured Pet*. Gloucestershire: Ringpress Books.

Milani, M. (1998) *Preparing for the Loss of Your Pet: Saying Goodbye with Love, Dignity, and Peace of Mind*. Roseville, CA: Prima Lifestyles.

Montgomery, H. and Montgomery, M. (1991) *Good-Bye My Friend: Grieving the Loss of a Pet*. Minneapolis, MN: Montgomery Press.

Nieburg, H.A. and Fisher, A. (1996) *Pet Loss: A Thoughtful Guide for Adults and Children*. Canada: HarperCollins Canada.

Peterson, L. (1997) *Surviving the Heartbreak of Choosing Death For Your Pet: Your Personal Guide for Dealing with Pet Euthanasia.* Tempe, AZ: Greentree Publishing.

Quackenbush, J. and Voith, V. (eds) (1985) *The Veterinary Clinics of North America, Small Animal Practice, Symposium on the Human-Companion Animal Bond.* Philadelphia, PA: W.B. Saunders Company.

Rosenberg, M.A. (1993) "Companion animal loss and pet owner grief." *AFRMA Rat & Mouse Tales.* March/June.

Sife, W. (1998) *The Loss of a Pet: A Guide to Coping with the Grieving Process When a Pet Dies.* New York, NY: Howell Book House.

Sussman, M. (ed.) (2003) *Pets and the Family.* New York, NY: Longman Publishing Group.

Tousley, M. (1997) *Final Farewell: Preparing for and Mourning the Loss of Your Pet.* Phoenix, AZ: Our Pals.

Wolfelt, A.D. (2004) *When Your Pet Dies: A Guide to Mourning, Remembering and Healing.* Collins, CO: Companion Press.

Children, loss and grief

Adamec, C. (1996) *When Your Pet Dies: Dealing with Your Grief and Helping Your Children Cope.* New York, NY: Berkley Publishing Group.

Buscaglia. L. (2002) *The Fall of Freddie the Leaf: A Story for All Ages.* New York, NY: Henry Holt and Company Inc.

Grollman, E.A. (1991) *Talking About Death: A Dialogue Between Parent and Child.* New York, NY: Beacon Press.

Heegaard, M.E. (2001) *Saying Goodbye to Your Pet: Children can Learn to Cope with Pet Loss.* Minneapolis, MN: Fairview Press.

Jarratt, C.L. (1994) *Helping Children Cope with Separation and Loss.* Boston, MA: Boston, MA: Harvard Common Press.

Morehead, D. and Cannon, K. (1996) *A Special Place for Charlee: A Child's Companion Through Pet Loss.* Beaver Dam, WI: Partners in Publishing. (Reading age 4–8)

Rogers. F. (2002) *When A Pet Dies.* New York, NY: Paperstar. (Reading age 4–8)

Rylant, C. (2002) *Dog Heaven.* New York, NY: Scholastic US. (Reading age 0–preschool)

Viorst, J. (1971) *The Tenth Good Thing About Barney.* New York, NY: Simon and Schuster. (Reading age 4–8)

Wolfelt, A.D. (1983) *Helping Children Cope with Grief.* Muncie, IN: Accelerated Development.

The grief process, self help

Baumgardner, B. (2002) *A Passage Through Grief.* Nashville, TN: Broadman and Holman Publishers.

Davies, P. (1989) *Grief: Climb Toward Understanding: Self-Help When You are Struggling.* Queensland: Sunnybank Publishers.

Deits, B. (1992) *Life After Loss: A Personal Guide Dealing with Death, Divorce, Job Change, and Relocation.* Tucson, AZ: Fisher Books.

James, J.W. (1998) *The Grief Recovery Handbook.* Canada: HarperCollins Canada.

Levine, S. (1989) *Healing into Life and Death.* New York, NY: Doubleday.

Lightner, C. and Hathaway, N. (1991) *Giving Sorrow Words: How to Cope with Grief and Get on with Your Life.* New York, NY: Warner Books.

Manning, D. (1984) *Don't Take My Grief Away: What to do When You Lose a Loved One.* Canada: HarperCollins Canada.

Rando, T.A. (1991) *How to Go on Living When Someone You Love Dies.* New York, NY: Bantam Books.

Ross, C.B. and Sorensen, J.B. (1998) *Pet Loss and Human Emotion: Guiding Clients Through Grief.* Washington, DC: Hemisphere Publishing Corporation.

Staudacher, C. (1987) *Beyond Grief: A Guide for Recovering from the Death of a Loved One.* Oakland, CA: New Harbinger Publishers.

Staudacher, C. (1991) *Men and Grief: A Guide for Men Surviving the Death of a Loved One.* Oakland, CA: New Harbinger Publishers.

Tatelbaum, J. (1984) *Courage to Grieve: Creative Living, Recovery and Growth through Grief.* Canada: HarperCollins Canada.

Loss and grief counseling

Kübler-Ross, E. (1975) *Death: The Final Stage of Growth.* New York, NY: Macmillan General Reference.

Kübler-Ross, E. (1997) *On Death and Dying.* New York, NY: Simon and Schuster.

Rando, T.A. (1984) *Grief, Dying and Death: Clinical Interventions for Caregivers.* Ottawa, Canada: Research Press.

Smart, D., Welch, D. and Zawistoski, R. (1991) *Encountering Death: Structural Activities for Death Awareness.* Muncie, IN: Accelerated Development.

Wolfelt, A.D. (1992) *Understanding Grief: Helping Yourself Heal.* Abingdon: Taylor and Francis.

Worden, W.J.W. (1982) *Grief Counseling and Grief Therapy: A Handbook for the Mental Health Practitioner.* New York, NY: Springer Publishing Company.

Helpful organizations

American Association of Human–Animal Bond Veterinarians
www.ahhabv.org

Anthrozoology Institute
University of Southampton
University Road
Southampton
England SO17 1BJ
Tel: + 44 (0) 2380595000
www.soton.ac.uk

Association for Pet Loss and Bereavement
PO Box 106
Brooklyn
NY 11230
Tel: 718-382-0690
www.aplb.org

Delta Society
875 124 Avenue NE
Suite 101
Bellevue
WA 98005
Tel: 425-226-7357

Delta Society Australia
Suite 706
74 Pitt Street
Sydney
Australia
Tel: 0292313218

**Equine Assisted Growth and Learning
Association (EAGALA)**
PO Box 993
Santaquin
UT 84655
Tel: 877-858-4600
www.eagala.org

Society and Animals Forum
PO Box 1297
Washington Grove
MD 20880-1297
Tel: 301-963-4751
www.psyeta.org

Therapet Animal Assisted Therapy Foundation
15632 Hwy 110
Suite 7
Whitehouse
TX 75791
Tel: 903-839-1201
www.therapet.com

Therapy Dogs International Inc.
88 Bartley Road
Flanders
NJ 07836
Tel: 973-252-9800
www.tdi-dog.org

Index